Sheridan
and the Drama of Georgian England

BOOKS BY JOHN LOFTIS

AS AUTHOR:

Steele at Drury Lane
Comedy and Society from Congreve to Fielding
The Politics of Drama in Augustan England
The Spanish Plays of Neoclassical England
With M. G. Jones, R. Southern, and A. H. Scouten,
The Revels History of Drama in English, Vol. 5

AS EDITOR

Richard Steele, *The Theatre*
With V. A. Dearing, *The Works of John Dryden*, Vol. 9
Restoration Drama: Modern Essays in Criticism
Nathaniel Lee, *Lucius Junius Brutus*
Joseph Addison, *Essays in Criticism and Literary Theory*

AS GENERAL EDITOR

The Regents Restoration Drama Series
(thirty-two volumes)

John Loftis

SHERIDAN
and the Drama of
Georgian England

HARVARD UNIVERSITY PRESS

Cambridge, Massachusetts

1977

This book is for my daughters,
Mary, Laura, and Lucy.

Contents

Preface

Referring to the art in which she excelled, the actress Sarah Siddons emphasized 'the quality of abstraction', a quality recurrent in Sheridan's art as a dramatist. 'Abstraction'—that is, as the *Oxford English Dictionary* puts it, the 'withdrawal, separation or removal' of something from the whole in which it originated. Mrs. Siddons alluded to the need for an actor or actress to isolate and in so doing emphasize traits or emotions in the character portrayed. The result in her own performances—as in those of her famous brother John Philip Kemble—was a stylization in which a dominant impression took precedence over emotional range. In their roles in *Pizarro*, the nature of the play permitted Mrs. Siddons and her brother to 'abstract' tragic emotions. An earlier generation of actors and actresses had portrayed very different emotions in Sheridan's comedies, his comic opera, and his farce, but the process of stylization, of emphasizing dominant qualities in dramatic characters with a corresponding inattention to emotional subtleties, had been required by the nature of Sheridan's work in the 1770s no less than in that of the 1790s.

Like a caricaturist in the graphic arts, Sheridan isolates, emphasizes, and—in his earlier and more important work—ridicules his characters and the conventional dramatic situations in which he places them. Although his comedies and his comic opera bear the marks of his admiration for the Restoration dramatists, they are thoroughly of their time, resembling the plays of his Georgian predecessors. Yet however closely he followed his predecessors, to describe *The Rivals*, *The Duenna*, *The School for Scandal*, and *The Critic* as derivative would be to ignore the strategy of literary burlesque he employs. He repeats dramatic formulae at least as old as the Restoration, but he does it with such audacity that theatrical commonplaces acquire originality of impact.

This is a book about Sheridan and also a book about Georgian drama, of which Sheridan's comedies, opera, and farce are the finest expression. Not many Georgian comedies except those of Goldsmith and Sheridan are known even to specialists in eighteenth-century literature—and the result has been a faulty understanding of that enigmatic literary phenomenon 'sentimentalism' and of Sheridan's relationship to the drama of his time. Sheridan surpassed his older contemporaries, not by innovation in the theory of comedy, but by his sensitivity to the rhythms of prose dialogue and by his capacity to give familiar dramatic situations intensified force by his mastery of the techniques of burlesque.

Writing this short book has proved to be a most agreeable task, and I thank the General Editors of the Series in which it appears, Kenneth Richards and Peter Thomson, as well as J. K. D. Feather of Basil Blackwell and Mott, Ltd., for suggesting that I do so and for their informed criticism of my work. I am grateful to Norman Philbrick, who gave me access to the resources of his library and with generosity of time provided expert advice at all stages of my work. I thank Carl Maves for calling my attention to stylistic infelicities. I owe special thanks to my long-time editorial and research assistant, Mrs. Carol B. Pearson, whose help has enabled me to complete the book during years when my teaching and administrative duties have been uncommonly demanding.

As my notes reveal, I owe much to the published work of my predecessors—above all, to that of the foremost authority on Sheridan of our time, Professor Cecil Price, who has published an edition of the *Dramatic Works* that may justly be considered 'definitive'. My quotations from Sheridan are based on this edition. Professor Price includes extensive quotations from the early reviews of Sheridan's works. However, except in instances in which I include a note referring to Price's edition—or to one of several other books that reprint relevant reviews—I base my quotations on my own transcriptions from the files of eighteenth-century newspapers preserved in the British Museum.

I gratefully acknowledge permission to reprint, in modified form, several paragraphs from the introduction to my edition of *The School for*

Scandal (1966) in the Crofts Classics Series, AHM Publishing Corporation; and to reprint, again in modified form, a portion of my essay on *Pizarro*, published in *Eighteenth-Century Studies*, VIII (1975), by the American Society for Eighteenth-Century Studies.

JOHN LOFTIS
STANFORD, CALIFORNIA
FEBRUARY 1976

I

Introduction

In our part of the twentieth century, attitudes towards Sheridan are curiously divided. There is a broadly based though tacit assumption that he is a major dramatist. *The Rivals* and *The School for Scandal* are performed more frequently by professional companies, I believe, than any other English play of the eighteenth century. Goldsmith's *She Stoops to Conquer* may surpass one or the other of them in total number of productions, but only because of its suitability for drama groups in the schools. *The Critic* retains the popularity on stage it has had since it was written. There are other measures of Sheridan's present reputation. Discoveries of new manuscripts of his plays cause excitement in Britain and America. As national treasures, they can be exported from Britain only with the approval of an agency of government. In Britain as in the United States they command high prices. Sheridan's dramatic works have been edited with the skill and with the amplitude of editorial apparatus reserved for major writers.[1] His letters have been edited in similar fashion[2]—though this is perhaps as much a tribute to his social and political prominence as to his prestige as a dramatist.

Yet when we turn from the professional theatre and the literary market place to recent drama criticism, we find Sheridan's reputation sharply reduced. The reservations about him have largely been conveyed by silence. Few essays are devoted to his five-act comedies.[3] I would guess that the editors of journals which print interpretative articles about the drama receive five or ten contributions on Congreve—and perhaps nearly as many on Etherege and Wycherley—for every one on Sheridan. Certainly an editor of an anthology of modern criticism of eighteenth-century drama would be hard pressed to give representation to Sheridan compatible with his importance. But if most scholars have chosen to ignore him, several have presented a plausible case against him.

Why the recent devaluation of the comedies by critics and historians of the drama? Matters have not always been so.

Even before the appearance of *The School for Scandal*, Samuel Johnson, Sheridan's senior by forty-two years, praised him highly.[4] David Garrick, whose regard for *The Rivals* and *The Duenna* influenced his decision to aid Sheridan in purchasing a share in the proprietorship of Drury Lane Theatre, 'attended the rehearsals of the School for Scandal', James Boaden reports, 'and openly announced the brilliant diction of the play'.[5] Lord Byron, who in his youth knew Sheridan in his age, refers in his letters to Sheridan's plays in a manner that implies regard for them as classics which educated men would know. Byron's 'Monody on the Death of . . . Sheridan', spoken from the stage at Drury Lane, praises the comedies ('The matchless dialogue, the death-less wit') as well as Sheridan's triumphs in Parliamentary oratory. William Hazlitt, in his Lectures on the *English Comic Writers* (published in 1819), refers to *The School for Scandal* as 'if not the most original, perhaps the most finished and faultless comedy which we have'.[6] Late in the nineteenth century Sir Henry Irving again used superlatives in an assessment of Sheridan's achievement:

> Sheridan brought the comedy of manners to the highest per-
> fection, and *The School for Scandal* remains to this day the most
> popular comedy in the English language. Some of the characters
> both in this play and in *The Rivals* have become so closely asso-
> ciated with our current speech that we may fairly regard them as
> imperishable. No farce of our time has so excellent a chance of
> immortality as *The Critic*.[7]

The writings of George Henry Nettleton, the leading American authority on Sheridan of the last generation, imply that there was no major change in critical opinion until some years after the First World War.[8]

The number of editions and stage productions of the plays testifies to Sheridan's popularity. The editions are too numerous to count, but a glance at the entries for them in a large library is persuasive. Owing to the researches of Charles Beecher Hogan, we have a statistical record of the performances of the plays in the last quarter of the eighteenth century.[9] *The School for Scandal* was the most frequently performed of all plays; *The Duenna* followed in fourth place; and among the after-pieces *The Critic* was in tenth place. No doubt Sheridan's position as a proprietor of Drury Lane and, beginning in the 1780s, his prominence as a political figure had something to do with the frequency of performances, but we can be sure that the plays found appreciative audiences. Even *Pizarro*, the anticlimatic coda to Sheridan's dramatic career, had a run that is legendary.

If the comedies of Sheridan have held the stage even until the present with more tenacity than any others of their time, there is a case against them, though as I have suggested it has seemed more compelling to scholars than to theatre audiences. The case has been cogently argued by Mr. Marvin Mudrick and, more recently, by Mr. A. N. Kaul.

In an essay, 'Restoration Comedy and Later', read at a meeting of the English Institute in 1954, Mr. Mudrick writes as an evaluative critic, differentiating the achievements of comic dramatists in several periods.[10] Although primarily concerned with the Restoration dramatists, he writes about others, including Sheridan. After analysis of and praise for Congreve, Mr. Mudrick continues in a sterner vein:

> It is by now safe to assert that Sheridan . . . had a passive audience and no cult of manners; that this audience, bottle-fed on sermons and sentimental comedy, refused to recognize entire continents of vitality; that sex was inadmissible and irony incomprehensible; that good nature—which tended to be defined, dramatically, as an incapacity for thought—had replaced good manners; that Sheridan, the presumptive inheritor of the tradition of Congreve, found his inheritance dissipated before he could lay his hands on it, and was in fact writing, not comedies of manners, but—patched out with hasty reconstructions of Jonsonian and Restoration types—good natured sentimental dramas of comic intrigue and situation, which Fielding had acclimated to fiction, in the guise of anti-sentimentalism, a generation before.

I do not think that 'It is by now [or was in 1954] safe to assert' the validity of all the charges in Mr. Mudrick's bill of complaints. Is it true that Sheridan, who wrote his comedies during Samuel Johnson's later years, 'had a passive audience and no cult of manners?' Does not a reading of Boswell's *Life* provide convincing evidence to the contrary?

I do not understand what Mr. Mudrick means when he describes Sheridan's audience as 'bottle-fed on sermons and sentimental comedy'. Is there any solid evidence that the audience heard more sermons than the audience of a hundred years earlier? I think not. There is even less reason to believe that the Georgian audience was 'bottle-fed' on 'sentimental comedy'. Shakespeare was the dramatist whose plays were most frequently performed. Even if we confine attention to the new comedies of mid-century, we can describe the larger number of them as 'sentimental' only at the risk of confounding distinctions between plays that are very unlike one another in subject, tone, structure, and didactic strategy. I agree with Mr. Mudrick that the dramatists 'refused to recognize entire continents of vitality'. The limitation of the subjects of comedy to the love intrigues and matrimonial problems of the gentry is indeed a major liability. Even so, it is a liability that Georgian shares with Restoration comedy. Sex was not exactly 'inadmissible' in the comedy of Sheridan's era, as Lady Teazle's near approach to adultery will remind us, but Mr. Mudrick certainly is right to the extent that the dramatists were severely limited in the portrayal of sexual relationships, as the Restoration dramatists were not, by the inhibitions of their audiences. As for the summary judgement that Sheridan 'found his inheritance dissipated before he could lay his hands on it', I find Mr. Mudrick's metaphors difficult to understand. But insofar as he means that Sheridan's comedies are damaged by the presence in them of stock characters, character-relationships, and subjects taken over from earlier drama, I disagree. On the contrary, I believe, as I shall explain, that some of Sheridan's best scenes succeed by reason of exaggeration to the point of burlesque of situations taken from Restoration comedy.

Mr. Kaul, whose discussion of Sheridan is a brief interlude in a far-ranging book, *The Action of English Comedy* (1970),[11] cites Mr. Mudrick approvingly, and he writes about Sheridan in a similar vein. Several of his remarks will repay quotation as succinct expressions of widely-held opinions. 'The place of Sheridan', he writes, '... is not difficult to define. It is not an important place; quite obviously he originates nothing of any importance, and he leads nowhere. More markedly than Goldsmith, he is a backward-looking dramatist.' Insofar as this is an historical assessment of Sheridan's relationship to his predecessors and successors rather than an evaluation of Georgian comedy and Sheridan's personal accomplishment, I find much in Mr. Kaul's remarks convincing. Yet surely he oversimplifies when he writes, referring to a prologue to *The Rivals* Sheridan addressed to the personification of comedy, that the question at the time of that play (1775)

> was hardly whether the Muse of Comedy was to be displaced from the stage, since she was in fact virtually defunct there; it was whether anything at all could be done to displace the other—the 'Goddess of the woful countenance'—who had long usurped the theater as her own exclusive realm.

This is to underestimate Sheridan's Georgian predecessors, with whose comedies I shall be concerned in the next chapter.

Mr. Kaul presents clearly and simply the traditional conception of mid-century dramatic history—a conception that has now been discredited by, among others, Mr. Robert D. Hume.[12] Avoiding metaphorical language (which can obscure historical reality), Mr. Hume examines in close, at times statistical, detail the comedies first performed between 1760 and 1773. I think his analysis fully supports his conclusion, which I quote:

> Despite the development of interest in various sorts of 'sentimental' plays during the 1760's, Goldsmith and Sheridan inherited a thriving comic tradition which continued full blast around them. Murphy, Foote, Macklin, Colman, and Garrick made a very considerable group indeed. To say that Goldsmith and Sheridan represent a 'return' to earlier modes is to ignore the the huge amounts that they took from the thriving comic theater of their own time.

Although I think Mr. Kaul's conception of mid-eighteenth-century comedy is inaccurate, I am concerned here with his evaluation of Sheridan—an evaluation distorted by overemphasis on an evolutionary view of the drama. We must of course consider the development—or evolution—of Georgian drama if we are to understand Sheridan's place and importance in English drama. Furthermore, Georgian drama is a subject worthy of study quite apart from Sheridan. Yet we must not allow attention to the history of drama to prejudice our evaluation of Sheridan's plays. It is perhaps true that he 'originates nothing of any importance' (except a distinction and precision in stage dialogue unequalled since 1660 except by Dryden and Congreve); it is true that 'he leads nowhere'. He was indeed 'a backward-looking

B

dramatist': any writer of literary burlesque must be. Burlesque sustains itself on its satirical targets. Our primary task should be an understanding and assessment of Sheridan's unique accomplishment, a task that can scarcely be performed without attention to what went before. *The School for Scandal* is a superb expression of the Georgian comic tradition. We can recognize it for what it is: not a lonely achievement, except that it is better than the other Georgian comedies of manners, but very much of its time. Yet the play deserves evaluation for what—in isolation—are its own qualities. It should not suffer in our esteem for what Sheridan and other dramatists failed to do later. Still less should it suffer from erroneous assumptions about the comedies other Georgian dramatists wrote.

The review of Cecil Price's edition of Sheridan's *Dramatic Works* in *The Times Literary Supplement*, 22 February 1974 (deservedly given the place of honour on the front page) has an apt title: 'Sheridan and the Art of Burlesque'. Many of the difficulties spectators or readers of the comedies experience in evaluating them would disappear if they recognized that Sheridan was above all a master of burlesque. To be sure, no one can fail to recognize that *The Critic* is a stage burlesque, and no one with a knowledge of dramatic history can fail to recognize its place in a well-defined tradition established by the Duke of Buckingham's *The Rehearsal* of 1671. Yet one can fail to recognize the component of burlesque in *The Rivals*, *The Duenna*, and *The School for Scandal*.[13] (Sheridan had no intention of writing burlesque in his operatic tragedy *Pizarro*; it is one of the ironies of his career that that strange play bears a distant resemblance to Mr. Puff's tragedy of 'The Spanish Armada'.)

Sheridan's strengths and his weaknesses, in some instances alleged weaknesses, are corollaries of his satirical techniques. His strengths relate to his concentration on isolated scenes or groups of scenes rather than on continuity. His strengths are, above all, precision of diction in dialogue that rapidly scores witty hits at aberrations of behaviour in social relationships; and, secondarily, skill in the construction of scenes that succeed on stage by reason of incongruities and surprises conveyed visually as well as verbally. His weaknesses, if such we choose to consider them, are again corollaries of his elaboration of episodes at the expense of their relationships to the whole. He was not interested in the cumulative development of his characters throughout a play nor indeed in the depiction of emotional subtleties in his characters. His characters are derivative in the sense that they have long literary ancestries, and the same is true of his plots. His concerns lay elsewhere: in the exaggeration of and variations on the traditional patterns of the comedy of manners in characterization and action.

Apart from *The Critic*, in which the mode of burlesque is self-evident, *The Rivals* is most patently a reworking with exaggeration of types of characters and oppositions between them that had been used and reused for upwards of a century. In *The Duenna* burlesque may be less prominent and in any event is more difficult to perceive because we are less familiar with the Restoration 'Spanish plots' and their eighteenth-century descendants than with the comedies of manners. Yet *The Duenna* follows with comic exaggeration conventions that can be traced as far back as Sir Samuel Tuke's *The Adventures of Five Hours*, first performed in 1663. So complex a play as *The School for Scandal* cannot be comprehensively described as a burlesque. However, the close resemblance between the first act of *The Critic* and the 'scandal scenes' of of the earlier play, as well as the characterization of Lady Sneerwell and her circle, assures us that in one of its dimensions *The School for Scandal* may be regarded as a burlesque.

The terminology of criticism has of course changed since the 1770s. Yet there has been remarkable consistency of opinion in the analytical description of Sheridan's achievements and omissions, notwithstanding the major changes in the critical evaluation of his plays. Even before the first public performance of *The School for Scandal* Garrick, using the metaphorical language of the eighteenth century, made an observation about two aspects of Sheridan's plays that still seems just. Along with praising the 'brilliant diction' of *The School for Scandal*, Garrick, according to James Boaden, compared Sheridan to Congreve—but tempered this high praise 'with something of reasonable regret, that like his great model, the writer should have less nature than wit'.[14] 'Less nature than wit'—less skills, that is, in creating characters who seem authentic representations of living persons than in writing controlled and witty dialogue. Garrick did not comment on Sheridan's habit of characterization by caricature. Yet such a comment may be latent in the comparison to Congreve. If *The Double Dealer* and *The Way of the World* include—along with characters that are caricatures—more complex characters than any we find in Sheridan, I am not convinced that the same can be claimed for *The Old Bachelor* and *Love for Love*.

Sheridan's plots, as I have implied, are in their derivatory quality corollaries of his intensity of focus on separate episodes and his fondness for burlesque. No doubt the haste with which he wrote, or, to be more precise, completed his plays had something to do with the limited originality of his plots. *The Duenna* resembles the English—and French —adaptions and translations of the Spanish comedies of intrigue.[15] *The Rivals* and *The School for Scandal,* in addition to their generalized similarities to earlier comedies of manners, resemble in certain characters and episodes specific mid-century comedies.

However hurriedly Sheridan may have completed his plays, he closes his intrigues neatly and with finality. He leaves no disturbing matrimonial or financial loose ends. The fifth act of *The School for Scandal* may be anticlimactic, as many have said. But the uncertainties in personal relationships are definitively resolved, even in the case of Sir Peter and Lady Teazle, where there is reason enough for an open ending of the sort we find in several of the best Restoration comedies. The tidiness of Sheridan's denouements reinforces the sense of emotional and social conservatism his plays convey. When he revised Vanbrugh's *The Relapse*, he removed the ambiguities, notably those having to do with Amanda's prospects for the future, and closed his own play, *A Trip to Scarborough,* with conventional reconciliations and marriages. He paid a price, in a diminished fidelity to authentic experience, for the manner with which he concluded his plays, and in our time that price has lowered his reputation.

Writing when he did, he faced severe restrictions in depicting sexual and matrimonial relationships. Unlike those of the Restoration, the theatrical audiences of the mid- and late eighteenth century had limited tolerance for the audacious dramatization of sexual emotion— of the kind, for example, we encounter in Dryden's *Marriage A-la-Mode.*[16] Not until the mid-twentieth century did an uninhibited portrayal of sexual feelings and relationships comparable to that in some of the Restoration comedies again become acceptable in plays performed in public theatres, a circumstance attesting the appropriateness of the title of Norman N. Holland's book about Etherege, Wycherley, and Congreve, *The First Modern Comedies.*[17] Audiences now, like those in the time of Charles II but not in that of George III, admire an analytical honesty in the representation of even the most private of experiences. Hence, I believe, one of the major reasons for the rise of Restoration comedy in the esteem of students of drama and the corresponding decline in their esteem for *The Rivals* and *The School for Scandal*. Put simply, we may say that Etherege, Wycherley, and Congreve now seem to many persons to be more honest than Sheridan in their dramatic commentaries on their subjects.

The position of Sheridan in our time is a corollary of our own predilections and hostilities. Sheridan shares with other men of genius who wrote in the late eighteenth century qualities which we find uncongenial.

He dramatizes fully and clearly, in prose that frequently rises to epigram but never to a Shakespearian kind of ambiguity,[18] relatively simple relationships among individuals and groups of individuals. We are never in doubt about his implied judgements of characters. He includes no such disturbing and enigmatic relationships as that between Mrs. Fainall and Mirabell in *The Way of the World*. He assumes a beneficent providence in which the compassionate and generous prevail over malicious schemers. He accepts the relationships among social classes as he and most of his contemporaries perceived them; he does not pose disturbing questions about social justice. His are benign comedies with a satirical bite that reaches only to fatuous and malicious individuals.

It has become necessary to argue that Sheridan is a 'major' dramatist —major, that is, unless we choose to reserve the adjective for the few who were supremely gifted. Yet he is less of an innovative dramatist than was commonly assumed before the Second World War. It is no longer possible to argue that, with Goldsmith, Sheridan laughed the Georgian theatre out of an enervating taste for 'sentimental' comedy. If the nature of Sheridan's relationship to his Georgian predecessors has not been fully explored, the researches of Arthur Sherbo, G. W. Stone, R. W. Bevis, and R. D. Hume, among others, have revealed that the mid-century audience had not lost a liking for laughing comedy.[19]

Nevertheless, in the study of Sheridan we cannot escape the ubiquitous and ambiguous adjective 'sentimental'. It is difficult to get on with the word; it is all but impossible to get on without it. I cannot avoid it, though I use it as sparingly as possible. It was often used from about the middle of the eighteenth century onwards, at first with approbatory but as time passed increasingly with derogatory connotations.[20] Sterne's use of it in the title of *A Sentimental Journey* is as ambiguous in its evaluative dimension as is the author's evaluation of Yorick's conduct on his travels. The word was used in a spectrum of meanings in the later eighteenth century, and it is used in a different spectrum of meanings today.

To avoid confusion we must first differentiate between two referents of the adjective 'sentimental': the one, a quality of emotional excess in literature of any period; the other, qualities of literature which in England began to be apparent in the late seventeenth century and became more prominent in the eighteenth century. The two meanings are related, and both are applicable to many eighteenth-century plays. But they are distinct, and only the second of them is applicable to the plays of Sheridan.

There is no incompatibility, as a reading of Sheridan's plays convinces us, between a comedy that dramatizes the emotional and ethical attitudes many of us are accustomed to associate with eighteenth-century sentimentalism, and a didactic comedy that evokes laughter and satirical perception by ridiculing persons who are vain, affected, foolish, or malignant. Sheridan resembles other Georgian dramatists in admiring compassion and benevolence and in avoiding erotic episodes. He is unlike some though not all of them in keeping pathetic situations out of his comedies. His best comedy, *The School for Scandal*, has an acerbity and a precision of phrase that set it apart. Still, Charles Surface, like Charles Oakly in Colman's *The Jealous Wife* and many others in eighteenth-century literature, wins his lady by qualities of the heart rather than by clarity of mind; and Lady Teazle undergoes a conversion to domestic harmony as sudden as that of Loveless in Cibber's *Love's Last Shift*.

Sheridan's comedies are consistently witty and they are often satirical; they are not oppressively genteel nor do they include pathetic characters. Yet they share many qualities with the plays and novels of the 'sentimentalists': an admiring toleration, even relish, for eccentric and imprudent characters; an assumption that a ready sympathy for distressed persons is preferable to a ready wit in conversation; an inclination to regard seemingly wicked persons as reclaimable; a tacit assumption that a kindly providence guides events to a prosperous conclusion for those characters who possess the gift of charity. Happy endings are conventional in comedy. Shakespeare himself did not scruple to manipulate events on behalf of his favoured characters. The ambiguous ending in earlier English comedy is largely confined to the Restoration. The uncertainties are gone in Sheridan, as in mid-century drama at large.

A firmly conceived moral vision of tolerant good sense and compassion controls Sheridan's comedies, a moral vision that we could call 'sentimental', but only—lest we increase confusion—if we remember that we refer to qualities common to much of the best literature of Georgian England.

2

Sheridan and his Georgian Predecessors

Soon after Sheridan in the autumn of 1776 became one of the proprietors of Drury Lane, the theatre revived three of Congreve's comedies with minor revisions intended to make them acceptable to the Georgian audience. Sheridan himself seems to have made the revision at the suggestion of Garrick. 'I have no doubt', Thomas Davies wrote in 1780, 'but that Mr. Sheridan, by his [Garrick's] advice, made some judicious alterations in Congreve's Old Batchelor, Love for Love, and the Way of the World. By retrenching some licentious expressions, and connecting by some slight additions, character and sentiment, he has saved those excellent plays from oblivion, which the extreme delicacy of a refined age, whose ears are become exceedingly chaste, could not endure.'[1] In February 1777, eleven years after Garrick's adaptation of Wycherley's *The Country Wife* as *The Country Girl*, the theatre produced Sheridan's *A Trip to Scarborough*, an adaption of Vanbrugh's *The Relapse*. And in May 1777 the theatre produced Sheridan's *The School for Scandal*, with its obvious resemblances to *The Way of the World*. All this suggests not only an extraordinary creative energy on the part of Sheridan but a continuity in the tradition of comedy deriving from the Restoration.

Continuity in a comic tradition, but also modification of it. For all his devotion to Restoration comedy—evident in his revivals of Congreve's plays, in his seeming imitation in *The School for Scandal* of Congreve's dialogue, and in his adaption of Vanbrugh's *The Relapse*—Sheridan followed patterns of characterization and plotting that were well established by his predecessors among the Georgian dramatists.

His plays demonstrate with unusual clarity how every writer is time bound, conditioned by the generation just preceding that into which he is born. At his best Sheridan is superior to his predecessors, above all in the stylistic quality of his dialogue. But his superiority does not derive from innovations in comic theory or in dramatic construction. He was close enough to his predecessors to be accused by hostile critics of plagiarism. His accomplishment would seem less an isolated phenomenon if we were in the habit of reading, not merely the plays of Goldsmith, but those of George Colman the Elder, David Garrick, Arthur Murphy, Samuel Foote, and even those of Hugh Kelly and Richard Cumberland.

The charges of plagiarism need not be taken seriously, but if we read, say, Colman's *Polly Honeycombe* along with *The Rivals*, and Murphy's *Know Your Own Mind* along with *The School for Scandal*, we can understand why they were made. The first act of *The Critic*, with its transparent caricatures of living persons, resembles in its satirical strategy the short plays of Samuel Foote, whose works include references to Sheridan's father and Elizabeth Linley, subsequently Sheridan's wife. Sneer's complaint, in the first act of *The Critic*, about the current criticism of a style in genteel comedy which is 'the true sentimental, and nothing ridiculous in it from the beginning to the end', is anticipated by a complaint of Hugh Kelly's sentimental dramatist Lady Rachel Mildew in *The School for Wives* that the theatre managers had rejected her play because 'the audiences are tired of crying at comedies; and insist that my Despairing Shepherdess is absolutely too dismal for representation' (I). A character in Murphy's *Know Your Own Mind* had referred to 'new comedies that make you cry, and tragedies that put you to sleep' (II). Sheridan's genial tolerance for eccentric characters is not unlike Kelly's or even Cumberland's. Although Cumberland is the Sir Fretful Plagiary of *The Critic*, Sheridan in *The School for Scandal* used a test situation in which an elderly and wealthy relative ascertains a young man's compassion and benevolence before endowing him with a fortune that is anticipated in Cumberland's most successful play, *The West Indian*. Sheridan wrote laughing and satirical comedies, but so did Garrick, Colman, Murphy, and Foote as well as Goldsmith.

If Sheridan succeeded beyond the measure of his contemporaries or Georgian predecessors, he was, as I have suggested, a man of his time, in the nature if not in the quality of his plays. His important work was produced in the mid- and late 1700s, at the end of and just after the Garrick era. The repertories of the mid-century theatres provide the backdrop for his achievements.

It will be profitable to look more closely at the comedies of the most popular dramatists of mid-century, Sheridan's predecessors and to some extent his teachers. Using *The London Stage* as a guide (and making allowances in the interpretations of the numbers of performances for the date at which some of the plays were written), these dramatists would seem to be Benjamin Hoadly, David Garrick, George Colman the Elder, Arthur Murphy, Richard Cumberland, Hugh Kelly, and Oliver Goldsmith.

Goldsmith's and Sheridan's preference for laughing comedy is not an isolated phenomenon, nor is their eminence so lonely as the makers of anthologies would have us believe. Many of the most frequently performed comedies of the Garrick era, old and new, are laughing, satirical comedies. Hoadly's *The Suspicious Husband*, Colman's *The Jealous Wife*, Colman and Garrick's *The Clandestine Marriage*, Murphy's *The Way to Keep Him* and *Know Your Own Mind*, and Foote's many short plays provide sufficient reminders that comic dramatists had not forgotten how to make their audiences laugh at absurdities of behaviour, This is not to deny that Kelly and Cumberland as well as others exploited to excess the benevolent sensibility of some of their characters; the satirical assaults on new developments in comedy were not unprovoked. But even Kelly and Cumberland, who were I think the primary targets of both Goldsmith and Sheridan in their arraignments of sentimental comedy, intentionally provided ludicrous characters and situations. 'The eighteenth-century plays that Goldsmith would apparently include under his designation of "Weeping Sentimental Comedy," 'Arthur Friedman has observed, 'were not designed to produce tears throughout; indeed all of them, as far as I know, limit themselves to a very few sentimental scenes.'[2] The eighteenth-century dramatists are less inclined to depict disturbing consequences of human depravity than their predecessors in the Restoration, and their emphasis on magnanimous responses to persons in distress often seems a falsification of human nature as we experience it, but they were not consistently so solemn as Goldsmith in his essay 'On the Theatre' and Sheridan in *The Critic* would seem to imply.

Sheridan and Goldsmith have been so frequently associated in

historical accounts of the drama—with good reason—that to clarify
Sheridan's relationship to his predecessors requires attention as well to
Goldsmith, to his statements about comic theory even more than to his
comedies. Although Goldsmith died the year before Sheridan's first
play was performed, his activities as dramatic critic and dramatist
brought attention to issues that are inextricably associated with
Sheridan's career. Goldsmith's disputes about the nature of comedy were
inherited by Sheridan. I have already suggested that the two men may
have had specific targets, Richard Cumberland and Hugh Kelly, as
well as more general ones, in their satirical assaults on 'sentimental'
comedy. They were alike in their objections to what they regarded as
contamination of the genre of comedy. They were not lone campaigners
for laughing comedy at a time when the sentimentalists enjoyed an
overwhelming ascendency,[3] but they were the most influential of the
campaigners, and they were so closely associated in time that reference
to Goldsmith and the dramatists of whose work he was critical is a
needed preliminary to an account of Sheridan's place in Georgian drama.

To the first edition of his *The Choleric Man* (a title ironically appropriate to the future 'Sir Fretful Plagiary'), Cumberland in 1775
prefixed a long and petulant dedicatory epistle addressed 'To Detraction', and on his title page he pointedly included the phrase 'A Comedy'.
In his dedicatory epistle he defended his conception of comedy from
Goldsmith's alleged assault on his earlier play, *The Fashionable Lover*,
performed and printed not long before Goldsmith's essay 'On the
Theatre' was published at the beginning of 1773. The essay was
published anonymously, and Cumberland may not have known the
identity of its author.[4] 'But there remains a word to be said,' Cumberland reminds Detraction, 'on some learned animadversions of yours,
entitled *An Essay on the Theatre*, in which you profess to draw a
Comparison between Laughing and *Sentimental Comedy*; and in which you
are pleased evidently to point some observations at my comedy of the
Fashionable Lover: You insinuate that every blockhead can write
Sentimental or pathetic Comedy. . . '. Amid his ill-tempered expostula-
tions, Cumberland undertakes a self-defence that in literary strategy had
been anticipated by Steele half a century before in the preface to
The Conscious Lovers. Cumberland, like Steele, appeals to precedent in
classical antiquity for the use of grave subjects in comedy. *The Choleric
Man*, like *The Conscious Lovers*, is based on a play by Terence; Cumberland, as Steele had done before him, cites the example of Terence as

authority for his own theory of comedy. Steele's reference to Terence, as well as his quotation of a relevant passage from a Latin treatise then thought to be by Cicero, is unobtrusive and tactful; Cumberland's parade of classical authorities is laboured to the point of pedantry. Writing of Greek new comedy, he refers to 'the fragments of *Menander*' and other writers, asserting that they 'consist of moral sententious passages, elegant in their phrase, but grave, and many of them . . . of a religious cast'. His dedicatory epistle, which includes a simplified and distorted history of Greek and Roman comedy, is intended to be a rebuttal to Goldsmith's brief remarks about the generic qualities of comedy.

Even if Cumberland did not know that Goldsmith was the author of the essay 'On the Theatre', he may have been prompted to the attack its 'Detraction' by the more explicit criticism of himself included in Goldsmith's 'Retaliation: A Poem Including Epitaphs on Some of the Most Distinguished Wits of this Metropolis', published about two weeks after Goldsmith died in April 1774 and some nine months before the epistle prefixed to *The Choleric Man* appeared in December.[5] The specifics of Goldsmith's caricature would explain Cumberland's classical emphasis in his reply:

> Here Cumberland lies having acted his parts,
> The Terence of England, the mender of hearts;
> A flattering painter, who made it his care
> To draw men as they ought to be, not as they are.
> His gallants are all faultless, his women divine.
> And comedy wonders at being so fine;
> Like a tragedy queen he has dizen'd her out.
> Or rather like tragedy diving a rout.
> His fools have their follies so lost in a croud
> Of virtues and feelings, that folly grows proud,
> And coxcombs alike in their failings alone,
> Adopting his portraits are pleas'd with their own.
> Say, where has our poet this malady caught,
> Or wherefore his characters thus without fault?
> Say was it that vainly directing his view,
> To find out mens virtues and findings them few,
> Quite sick of pursuing each troublesome elf,
> He grew lazy at last and drew from himself?[6]

In his *Memoirs* published many years later, Cumberland alluded to his 'gratitude for the epitaph he [Goldsmith] bestowed on me in his poem called Retaliation',[7] and it has subsequently been a matter of dispute whether he did indeed fail to perceive the irony in Goldsmith's lines.[8] The dedication to *The Choleric Man*, published the same year as 'Retaliation,' should remove any doubt on the subject. Of course Cumberland understood Goldsmith's intention; he was vain but he was no fool. In his defensive strategy, he acknowledged the substance of the charges in Goldsmith's poem while appealing to classical precedent in an effort to reinterpret the charges in his own favour. It was not an unequivocal disadvantage to be 'The Terence of England, the mender of hearts'.

I do not know whether Cumberland was justified in assuming that Goldsmith's 'On the Theatre' was primarily directed against *The Fashionable Lover*. Cumberland may have had information unavailable to us. Yet if what Goldsmith wrote is closely and circumstantially applicable to *The Fashionable Lover*, he phrased the essay as a generalized criticism of 'the Weeping Sentimental Comedy, so much in fashion at present'. Goldsmith's objection to the confounding of genres in 'this species of Bastard Tragedy' would equally apply to *The Conscious Lovers*, which was still prominent in repertory,[9] as well as to other plays, including those of Hugh Kelly. Whether Cumberland knew what he was talking about or not, *The Fashionable Lover* merits brief attention as a type of the comedy Goldsmith had in mind.

After references to literary precedent, Goldsmith describes

> a new species of Dramatic Composition [which] has been introduced under the name of *Sentimental* Comedy, in which the virtues of Private Life are exhibited, rather than the Vices exposed; and the Distresses, rather than the Faults of Mankind, make our interest in the piece. These Comedies have had of late great success, perhaps from their novelty, and also from their flattering every man in his favourite foible. In these Plays almost all the Characters are good, and exceedingly generous: they are lavish enough of their *tin* Money on the Stage, and though they want Humour, have abundance of Sentiment and Feeling. If they happen to have Faults or Foibles, the Spectator is taught not only to pardon, but to applaud them, in consideration of the goodness of their hearts; so that Folly, instead of being ridiculed,

is commended, and the Comedy aims at touching our Passions without the power of being truly pathetic.

If more of this than we sometimes remember could be applied to Goldsmith's own *She Stoops to Conquer*, it is more obviously relevant to *The Fashionable Lover*, a melodramatic play about treacherous intrigue in which the title character, a lord, is brought to repentance. Lord Abberville attempts to seduce—or rape—the virtuous heroine, Miss Aubrey, who in the absence of her father resides with a rich but corrupt merchant. The merchant, Mr. Bridgemore, wishes Lord Abberville to marry his daughter, and the efforts of Bridgemore and his family to accomplish the alliance reveal the snobbery of the lord, the gaucherie of the merchant's family, and their treachery to Miss Aubrey. The family drive her out of their house when she is innocently caught in a compromising situation for which Lord Abberville alone is responsible. In a situation reminiscent of Richardson's *Clarissa*, Miss Aubrey takes refuge in the house of a woman who is, though the girl does not know it, a procuress for Lord Abberville. She is rescued by Mortimer, the uncle of Tyrrel, the young man she loves, and by the kindly Scotsman Colin Macleod—a warm-hearted eccentric in the pastoral tradition, who like the title character of Cumberland's *West Indian* has instincts unperverted by urban sophistication. Benevolent providence intervenes in behalf of Miss Aubrey. Her father returns and and reveals that Mr. Bridgemore has taken money intended for her. Tyrrel wins her in marriage. Lord Abberville repents emphatically and at length, revealing his treachery to her. We can understand well enough why Cumberland would have been sensitive to Goldsmith's remarks about 'bastard tragedy.'

Cumberland was, and knew that he was, a leading writer of a form of comedy in which catastrophe rather than happy marriage would seem to be the logical result of the events depicted. His exploitation of pathos in his portrayal of passive and innocent characters, in his earlier *The Brothers* and *The West Indian* as well as in *The Fashionable Lover*, was excessive, and in order to save his heroines he was compelled to assume the existence of a benevolent providence controlling seeming accidents and the repentances of villains. He was not humourless, and intermingled with his moralistic platitudes he provided keenly observed glimpses of tensions within English society—as in his portrayal in *The Fashionable Lover* of the merchant's family attending a reception at the house of Lord Abberville, only to find that their host had rudely departed before they arrived. Cumberland was best, and he seems to have known that he was, in the depiction of benevolent and uninhibited characters who were outsiders in fashionable society. After his success with Belcour, the title character of *The West Indian*, he worked a variant on the character in Colin Macleod of *The Fashionable Lover*. In the 'Advertisement' prefixed to the latter play, he explained why he had done so, in a statement that helps to account for his neglect of the traditional subjects of the comedy of manners:

> The level manners of a polish'd country, like this, do not supply much matter for the comic muse, which delights in variety and extravagance; wherever therefore I have made any attempts at novelty, I have found myself obliged either to dive into the lower class of men, or betake myself to the out-skirts of the empire; the centre is too equal and refined for such purposes.

This is a comment that acquires irony when we recall that Lady Sneerwell and Mrs. Candour made their appearance later in the same decade.

The Fashionable Lover is not untypical of Cumberland, though it is patently inferior to *The West Indian*. Yet it is scarcely typical of the comedies in the repertories of the Georgian theatres, the new comedies as well as those surviving from earlier times. It differs in its melodramatic quality—in the intensity of the distresses which the heroine suffers and in the greater emphasis on the depravity of other characters. Even so, there are similarities with many plays of the era, including those of Goldsmith and Sheridan. Colin Macleod has at least a distant resemblance to Goldsmith's Tony Lumpkin, another benevolent eccentric outside London society who helps to rescue a distressed lady. Lord Abberville has more to repent than Sheridan's Lady Teazle, but his change of heart is scarcely more sudden and emphatic. Cumberland depicted fashionable London society with repugnance rather than with sustained irony, but his judgement of it is not unlike Sheridan's. And if Cumberland made heavier demands on a benevolent providence to put all right by play's end than most of the dramatists, he was not alone in tacitly assuming that virtuous and compassionate characters would somehow be protected.

The plays of Hugh Kelly, who may have been the other principal target of Goldsmith and Sheridan, are less melodramatic, and they represent a closer approach to a just balance between sentiment and satire—a closer approach, but not an equilibrium. For his mockery of excessive sensibility or 'delicacy' notwithstanding, he never escaped from the blandness that is the consequence of a refusal to face the consequences of human depravity. His comedies reveal the strength of the mid-eighteenth-century preoccupation with the analysis of personality: not in his case with conducting an original analysis of his own but rather with the dramatization of premises concerning benevolence which he took from earlier writers. Samuel Johnson commented on the current interest in tracing the springs of behaviour. 'The contest about the original benevolence or malignity of man had not yet commenced', Johnson wrote in 1765, in describing one of the advantages Shakespeare enjoyed over later dramatists. 'Speculation had not yet attempted to analyse the mind, to trace the passions to their sources, to unfold the seminal principles of vice or virtue, or sound the depths of the heart for the motives of action'.[10] Johnson recognized the complexity of the problems involved in any honest effort to do so, as Kelly, on the showing of his plays, did not. Whether from personal conviction or merely from a prudential desire to take advantage of literary fashion, he wrote plays exemplifying the 'original benevolence' of his characters.

His best play, *False Delicacy*, is in fact propelled by a succession of acts of benevolence, as several couples in turn find themselves blocked in their quest for the partners of their choice by their unwillingness to forsake other partners lest they cause them distress. No small amount of ingenuity on Kelly's part is required to delay until play's end the resolution of such insubstantial and self-inflicted difficulties. Kelly accomplishes it humorously, and not without ironic commentary on the failure of perception and good sense that produces the misunderstandings. Two of his characters, Mrs. Harley and Cecil, provide in their uninhibited and clearheaded commentary on the conduct of the others a rational norm by which the excesses in sensibility can be measured. Yet if the play is not an uncritical celebration of benevolence, it remains curiously remote from any experience we have had or can imagine other people to have had. It is oppressively genteel in its celebration of the decorums of fashionable society. And its easy assumptions about a protecting providence, summarized in the curtain speeches, are hollow. 'The stage should be a school of morality;' says Winworth, 'and the noblest of all lessons is the forgiveness of injuries.' To which

Rivers replies that 'the principal moral to be drawn from the transactions of to-day is, that those who generously labour for the happiness of others, will, sooner or later, arrive at happiness themselves.' Small wonder that Sheridan's Sneer, in the opening scene of *The Critic*, should allude to this exchange of platitudes.

False Delicacy was first performed in 1768 in competition with Goldsmith's *The Good Natured Man*, a play to which Kelly's bears closer resemblances than may at first appear. We prefer *The Good Natured Man*, of course, though in the strength of our preference we may be more strongly influenced than we are aware by the reputations of the two dramatists. In reading both plays, we have difficulty in arriving at a just sense of the authorial attitude toward the 'delicacy' of feeling and 'good nature' that is so prominent an attribute of their principal characters. Goldsmith's normative characters are prompter and more explicit than Kelly's in identifying the central satirical target: in *The Good Natured Man*, excessive, impractical, and undiscriminating benevolence, as it is practised by Honeywood, the title character. His uncle explains in the opening scene that 'he loves all the world; that is his fault.' The faithful servant Jarvis admits 'that he's rather too good natur'd; he's too much every man's man; that he laughs this minute with one, and cries the next with another.' Honeywood is a more convincing character than Kelly's lords and gentlemen, but his altruism, in his supreme act of generosity, is curiously like theirs: he is willing to surrender the girl he loves to a man he mistakenly believes has aided him in his financial reverses. Honeywood's errors of judgement notwithstanding, he does not emerge as a contemptible character. He is, like Yorick in Sterne's *Sentimental Journey*, subject to the 'ebbs and flows' of his humours, and, if he is imprudent, we can no more dislike him, or even disapprove of him, than we can of Yorick.

We need not bring *She Stoops to Conquer* into account to be convinced that Goldsmith was a better dramatist than Kelly. *The Good Natured Man* has thematic similarities to *False Delicacy* and is not unlike the latter play in moving on an overingenious plot. But Goldsmith has an advantage in that unlike Kelly his range of concerns transcends the manners and inhibitions of the rich and fashionable. Goldsmith objected, as he explained in his preface, to the limitation of comedy to the affairs of high society. He attempted to imitate the dramatists of the 'last age', he explained:

C

The term, *genteel comedy*, was then unknown amongst us, and
little more was desired by an audience, than nature and humour,
in whatever walks of life they were most conspicuous. . . .
Those who know any thing of composition, are sensible, that
in pursuing humour, it will sometimes lead us into the recesses
of the mean; I was even tempted to look for it in the master of
a spunging-house: but in deference to the public taste, grown of
late, perhaps, too delicate; the scene of the bailiffs was retrenched
in the representation. In deference also to the judgment of a
few friends, who think in a particular way, the scene is here
restored.[11]

Most of us too 'think in a particular way,' and we are likely to regard
the scene of Honeywood's confrontation with the bailiff come to
arrest him as an authenticating reminder of the realities of eighteenth-
century life—as a relief from the impression conveyed by too
many eighteenth-century comedies that only the rich need be taken
seriously.

Yet Kelly too in his later work broadened the range of his social and
moral concerns.[12] His later comedies, *A Word to the Wise* of 1770 and
The School for Wives of 1774, although emphatically 'genteel', are less
uniformly good natured than *False Delicacy*.

Consider *The School for Wives*, produced the year before Sheridan
made his reputation, a play that provides a vision of depravity in
fashionable London life not unlike that Sheridan provides in *The School
for Scandal*. Much of the action in Kelly's play is in intent at least
adulterous intrigue. Belville, an energetic and unscrupulous woman
chaser, bluntly explains his attitude toward his attractive wife (I.ii):
'. . . though I wou'dn't exchange Mrs. Belville's mind for any woman's
upon earth, there is scarcely a woman's person upon earth, which is
not to be a stronger object of attraction.' An experienced libertine
whose extra-marital affairs have been consummated before play's
opening, he makes two additional, and this time unsuccessful, attempts
on women, both attempts involving a measure of treachery. In an effort
to seduce a young innocent, Miss Leeson, who wishes to become an
actress, he pretends to be an Irish stage manager who can assist her to a
career. He fails, but he tries again with a guest in his own house,
Miss Walsingham, a high-spirited young woman who is the beloved
of one of his friends. This time he fails disastrously, and is mocked

and humiliated. Yet his profligacy notwithstanding, he appears as a not unamiable figure, and he is permitted the luxury of a fifth-act repentance and reconciliation with his wife. Kelly confronts the fact of depravity, not melodramatically in the manner of Cumberland, but with an acerbity not present in *False Delicacy*. Yet he retains his optimism about human nature and about providence. In the secondary action he enlarges his social vision to encompass the sympathetic portrayal of character types who had traditionally been objects of ridicule: the Irish and the lawyers. One old lawyer, in fact, reveals an unexpected generosity in endowing a young lawyer with a fortune for no good reason except an innate benevolence.

The comedies of Cumberland and Kelly, in some of their qualities at least, represent the type of drama of which Sheridan was critical, as Goldsmith had been before him. Other mid-century comedies prominent in the theatrical repertories reveal more clearly qualities characteristic of Sheridan's own comedies.

The popularity enjoyed by Benjamin Hoadly's *The Suspicious Husband* at both Drury Lane and Covent Garden lends importance to the play as a guide to and determinant of Georgian comic tradition. It is easy to understand why the play should have been popular; it is equally easy to understand why it is now seldom read. For if it is neatly constructed, combining a plot that produces suspense with scenes of lively conversational encounters, it is singularly innocent of attention to important human or social concerns. To be sure, the title character, Mr. Strictland, is afflicted with 'suspicion' that borders on paranoia. His defect of personality occasions the obstacles to be overcome not only by his wife but also by the young couples who have marriage in view. Yet Mr. Strictland's motiveless suspicion is merely assumed as a necessity of the plot, which turns on the intrigues of the unmarried young.

The play follows a pattern familiar in Restoration comedy: two young couples—one couple sprightly, the other grave—play out their courtships against cynical commentary provided by Ranger, a dissipated young rake, with opposition from 'the suspicious husband'. Mr. Strictland, guardian of Jacintha, refuses to countenance her desired marriage to Bellamy for the most conventional of reasons: she has a fortune of £30,000 and Bellamy an income of only £300 a year. The other girl, Clarinda, a houseguest of Mrs. Strictland, is free of Mr. Strictland's control, but his suspicions, abetted by mischance, complicate her romance with Frankly. The resemblance of all this to the pattern of Restoration comedy is intensified by the choral commentary on the folly of idealized love provided by Ranger, who in his first appearance on stage, reciting a love lyric after a sleepless night of dissipation, has more than a casual resemblance to Etherege's Dorimant in *The Man of Mode*.

In the nature and complexity of its intrigue, which includes a nocturnal encounter and near duel between Bellamy and Frankly outside of Mr. Strictland's house, the play resembles such Restoration 'Spanish plots' as Sir Samuel Tuke's *The Adventures of Five Hours* and Dryden's *An Evening's Love*. Hoadly in fact makes something like an acknowledgement of literary debt to the latter play by choosing two of the names of characters, Jacintha and Bellamy, Dryden had used. In a sequence of action for which there are many parallels in Spanish drama, Ranger, the roving, predatory male, climbs a ladder he finds placed against Mr. Strictland's house (placed there to aid Jacintha to elope) and finds himself in the dressing room of Mrs. Strictland. Her understandable alarm is intensified when she hears her husband coming. With good reason she avoids a confrontation by directing Ranger into an adjacent room, where he encounters the bewildered Jacintha. In making his escape from Mrs. Strictland's room, Ranger inadvertently leaves behind his hat—a threatening physical presence that, as Elizabeth Inchbald noted,[13] functions like a character in the play. The quick-witted women assisted by Ranger's good nature, avert disaster, and in the subsequent action Mr. Strictland, convinced that he has been excessively suspicious of his wife, acquiesces in the pairing off of the young couples.

In a play with such strong resemblances to Restoration comedy— to the comedy of manners in the characters and the relations between them; to the 'Spanish plots' in the busy intrigue—can we find qualities that are shared by the plays Sheridan wrote some thirty years later? Yes, emphatically. Sheridan's second play, *The Duenna*, is an operetta, but it is also a late-eighteenth-century rendering of a 'Spanish plot'. More of this later. What is relevant here is the firm evidence provided by *The Suspicious Husband* of the continued popularity of dramatic intrigue in the Spanish manner. Sheridan may or may not have looked back to Dryden and Tuke as he prepared *The Duenna* for the stage, but he could scarcely have been unaware of such a popular play as Hoadly's an intrigue play in the Georgian idiom. By the standards of his time, Hoadly is curiously tolerant of Ranger's libertinism, of his frank sexuality. Yet even Ranger reveals himself as an eighteenth-century man of feeling when he encounters Jacintha alone and at night. His preliminary effort ar seduction is met by tears, and he promptly learns that she is the beloved of his friend Bellamy. 'Her Tears affect me strangely' (III.iii), he says in an aside, altering his role at once to that of protector and confederate. His compassion and his good nature prevail, and so do similar qualities in the other characters—even finally in the irascible Mr. Strictland.

This is a genial play, lacking the cutting edge of satirical comedy, either that of the Restoration or that of Sheridan's 'scandal scenes'. In place of caustic conversational reviews of abberations, we have complexity of plot, fullness of incident. The exploitation of suspense caused by the presence of Ranger's hat in Mrs. Strictland's dressing room is not unlike that produced by Sheridan's manipulation of events in his 'screen scene', in each instance the audience perceiving the incriminating evidence in advance of the husband of the implicated lady.

Garrick was a dramatist of a lesser order of importance than Sheridan, and yet he anticipates Sheridan in his approach to his work: in his calculation of stage effect, in his willingness to rework old plays to make them acceptable to his audiences, in his interest in farce and burlesque as well as in five-act comedy. Neither man was an innovative theorist but rather a skilled and prudential playwright, writing to entertain the audiences of his day, accepting the inhibitions that kept disturbing and audacious sexual themes out of comedy. Like Sheridan, Garrick wrote with a benign conception of the human condition, and yet he was as firmly convinced as his successor at Drury Lane that the genres of comedy and tragedy should not be confounded.[14]

Two of his plays, I think, have a particular relevance to Sheridan's work: not as literary sources except in the most generalized sense but rather as expressions of literary and theatrical attitudes that conditioned plays by Sheridan. *A Peep Behind the Curtain* is a mid-century anticipation of *The Critic* in the restricted sense that it is a theatre manager's burlesque review of the routine problems of his business. *The Country Girl* is an adaptation of Wycherley's *The Country Wife* constructed on principles analogous to those controlling Sheridan's adaptation of Vanbrugh's *The Relapse* as *A Trip to Scarborough*.

A Peep Behind the Curtain, one of the most popular plays of its time,[15] resembles the other stage burlesques of the century following *The Rehearsal* in structure and in satirical strategy. A framing action encompasses a rehearsal, in this instance not of a play but of a burletta; both framing action and rehearsal include transparent references to theatrical personalities. Its success in the theatre notwithstanding, it is unimpressive in comparison with *The Critic*, lacking Sheridan's aphoristic phrases and his generalized commentary on authorial arrogance. Yet it represents the continuing tradition of stage burlesque in which Sheridan worked, and it is a Drury Lane play, written by his predecessor in the theatre. Like Sheridan after him, Garrick glances at current criticism of himself: here, the charges that he meddled with the plays of other authors. 'Was this your plot, Mr. Glib?', asks Lady Fuz, who has come to the rehearsal of 'The Burletta of Orpheus', 'Or your contrivance, Mr. Manager?' And the author answers in indignation that would not be inappropriate to Sir Fretful Plagiary: 'No, upon my soul, 'tis all my own contrivance, not a thought stole from Ancient or Modern; all my own plot.' In fact, Lady Fuz had referred, not to the trivial plot of the burletta, but to the 'plot' of a young man to elope with her daughter. All this resembles the first act of *The Critic*, in which charges of plagiarism and managerial interference are principal satirical targets.

The decorum of the Georgian theatre forbade any such pungent assault on sexual hypocrisy as Wycherley had made in *The Country Wife*. In reworking the play Garrick was driven to major omission and major alteration. *The Country Girl* testifies to the strength of sexual inhibition in the theatre of mid-eighteenth-century England. The inhibition had sufficient force to make the character Horner unaccept-able. How, we may ask in wonder, could Garrick have had the temerity to undertake an adaptation of *The Country Wife* if he had to omit the character whose famous stratagem to achieve unlimited sexual delight propels the plot? Yet in limited measure Garrick succeeded, and he did so by reverting to a play from which Wycherley had also taken suggestions, Molière's *L'École des femmes*. The detail is worth consider-ing for the insight it can provide into the affinities between Molière's comedies and those written in Georgian England—by Sheridan, among others. *The School for Scandal* recalls *L'École des femmes* in more than the 'School' of its title.

Molière's plays were frequently imitated, adapted, or performed in translation.[16] Goldsmith refers, in *The Bee*, to performances of comedies by Molière at each of the two patent houses in 1759, and in the preface to *The Good Natured Man* of 1768 he refers to Molière as providing a standard of excellence in comedy. 'Indeed the French comedy is now become so very elevated and sentimental', he writes, and his remark has relevance to English comedy as well, 'that it has not only banished humour and *Moliere* from the stage, but it has banished all spectators too.' Molière could provide a model for Goldsmith and for Garrick, Sheridan, and others, as the Restoration dramatists could not, because in addition to his many other achievements his comedies were chaste. 'The decency of the French stage', Thomas Davies writes in his account of Garrick's adaptation of Wycherley, 'and the profligacy of our own [during the Restoration], may be marked out in this area; for the Country Wife was evidently taken from L'Ecole des Femmes of Moliere, a comedy written upon the most simple plan, and worked up with wonderful skill, by that excellent comedian.'[17]

Garrick's problem in reworking *The Country Wife* under the monumental disadvantage of dispensing with Horner was to find a workable complication of his plot that could permit him to retain many of the episodes and character relationships of Wycherley's play. He solved it by transforming Mr. Pinchwife into an English equivalent of Arnolphe, an elderly guardian of the country girl who has had her reared in ignorance and innocence so that she would become a compliant wife. Because the guardian, now named Moody, is not yet married to the girl, though he pretends to be, the young gallant in pursuit of her can carry on his stratagems honourably and with marriage in view. Much of the intrigue of the latter part of Wycherley's play, including the old man's unsucessful attempt to disguise the girl and his abortive attempt to manipulate her exchange of letters with the importunate gallant, remains, and so does the secondary action involving Harcourt's and Sparkish's competive courtship of Alithea. But the 'china scene' could not survive, nor could the word play that in *The Country Wife* emphasizes sexual hypocrisy.[18] Garrick's play is a more radical alteration of its original than is Sheridan's *A Trip to Scarborough*, and it is less successful, but it represents an analogous effort to render the wit of a Restoration comedy acceptable to a Georgian audience.

In the afterpiece *Polly Honeycombe* (1760), George Colman anticipates even more closely than Garrick a central motif in a play of Sheridan's, in this instance *The Rivals*. Sheridan's Lydia Languish bears a strong resemblance to Colman's title character, like Lydia a female quixote. I shall defer examination of the likenesses—and differences—between the two characters, and their relationships to the literary tradition of the female quixote, until the next chapter. Here I shall consider the play Colman wrote the year after *Polly Honeycombe*, this one a full-length comedy and the most successful play of his career.

Crowded with forcefully conceived characters who move in a busy and complicated plot, *The Jealous Wife* like *Polly Honeycombe* suggests Colman's preoccupation with the novel. In an 'Advertisement' prefixed to the first edition, Colman acknowledges that it resembles *Tom Jones*: 'The Use that has been made in this Comedy of *Fielding's* admirable Novel of *Tom Jones*, must be obvious to the most ordinary Reader.' True enough, though *The Jealous Wife* is far from being a dramatization of the novel; it has lines of action, including that from which the title is drawn, which have no parallel in Fielding.

Yet the characters depicted—a country squire who cares more about his horses and his dogs than the young woman who is offered to him in marriage, a scheming lady of high society, an affected lord whose approaches to the heroine border on attempted rape, a venal and unscrupulous recruiting officer, as well as the young couple whose troubled progress to matrimony provides the organizing principle—all these remind us of Fielding. Harriot, as spirited and resourceful as Fielding's Sophie, leaves her father's house to escape from an impossible marriage to the well-named Sir Harry Beagle, taking refuge in the London house of her aunt Lady Freelove. With Lady Freelove's connivance, Lord Trinket insults her, and at a crucial moment in her distresses, Charles Oakly, her own Tom Jones, fails her: not by succumbing to another woman but rather to the bottle. When Harriot turns for shelter to Charles's uncle and guardian, complications arise from the absurd suspicions of the uncle's wife, the 'jealous wife' of the title. By some lucky and comical accidents, in which Lord Trinket's plan to remove Charles through impressment into the Navy is frustrated, the young lovers are brought together—with the blessing of Harriot's father when he discovers that the husband he had chosen for her has 'traded' her for a horse.

Like Fielding, Colman escapes from the blight of gentility that mars too much of eighteenth-century literature. The characters are chosen from the well born and rich, to be sure, but they are singularly free of a preoccupation with social decorum. Colman writes with a satirist's attention to absurdities of behaviour, above all that of the 'jealous wife'. Yet his evaluations of his characters turn on their qualities of heart, and it may not be an accident that he is most severe with the character of highest rank, Lord Trinket. Harriot's situation approximates those of other distressed virgins in eighteenth-century drama, but she has none of the passivity which often makes those characters objects of pity. Charles Oakly's failings anticipate those of Charles Surface just as they resemble those of their common ancestor Tom Jones, and they are forgiven for similar reasons. The love of Charles and Harriot has less of financial calculation in it than is customary in the matchings of Restoration comedy. Theirs is no misalliance, and yet, for Harriot at least, the marriage involves financial sacrifice. The point is worth noting, I think, because it is a symptom of the difference in emotional tone of eighteenth-century as opposed to Restoration comedy. Love counts for more in the marriage settlements of Georgian comedy.

Like Colman, Arthur Murphy may be recognized as one of the principal determinants of the Georgian conception of comedy inherited by Sheridan. Like others of his time, he admired, adapted, and—in some measure—imitated the comedies of Molière. Murphy's *The Way to Keep Him* (1760 and, in revised form, 1761), among the most popular comedies at Drury Lane under Garrick's management, could be considered a 'thesis' play in the manner of Molière, so neatly is it organized as a dramatization of tensions which disrupt married life and as an exposition of the means to correct them. It is satirical in didactic strategy, Murphy depicting complementary kinds of marital maladjustment: that of Lovemore, who as we could guess from his name suffers from boredom with his wife and desire for adulterous intrigue; and that of Sir Benjamin Constant, who is indeed 'constant' to the wife he loves even while fearing that his unfashionable devotion to her will make him ridiculous in London society. The play moves through a succession of extra-marital intrigues, approaching though never reaching adultery, to a denouement of reconciliation in which Sir Benjamin perceives the danger caused by his affectations and Lovemore suffers humiliation in his pretensions to an attractive widow. Murphy's title alludes to the education of Lovemore's wife, who learns that the way to keep her husband requires a return to the liveliness of spirit with which she had first attracted him.

If Murphy is more explicit and emphatic in recommending matrimonial fidelity than most of the late seventeenth-century dramatists had been, he yet writes in a pattern that is a recognizable extension from Restoration comedy: in his satirical conception of his carefully named characters, in his focus on the love affairs of the gentry, in the nature of the episodes which complicate his slender plot lines, and even in the texture of his dialogue. He did not achieve the unexpected turns of phrase that delight us in Congreve, yet let us remember that, except perhaps for Dryden, no other Restoration dramatist did so either. Murphy wrote wit dialogue that is more than competent, and it was spoken in the theatre by such superb actors as Garrick, Mrs. Cibber, and Mrs. Clive. The play, even in its limitations, reminds us of Restoration comedies: in its focus on a narrow range of the experience of persons from a narrow range of English society and in its avoidance of topics that do not impinge on the love or matrimonial affairs of the gentry. The play is coherent, well contrived, and witty, but like many earlier plays it may finally in its subject approach the parochial. To call it 'sentimental' is, I think, meaningless unless we are prepared to apply the word to nearly all eighteenth-century literature that accepted Christian morality as the principal criterion for judging character and action. It does not include pathetic characters nor does it assault our sympathies. Yet the firm moral basis of the play has as a corollary an absence of the emotional ambivalence—the ambivalence that we recognize from our own experience as an authenticating quality—of several of the best Restoration comedies.

These dramatists, Hoadly, Garrick, Colman, Murphy, Goldsmith, Cumberland, and Kelly, wrote the most popular full-length comedies of mid-century. Insofar as the conception of 'tradition' in Georgian comedy has relevance to the work of Sheridan, it is to the plays of these men that we should look to find it. Their plays were heterogeneous in nature and quality, and yet it may be profitable to venture some generalizations about them, as well as some comparisons between them and the Restoration comedies that Sheridan admired and, in one instance, reworked. The two eras in drama are separated by a century in time, by revolution in government, by growth in overseas commerce, by the dramatic reform movement, by the Stage Licensing Act—and yet there is a discernible line of continuity between Etherege,

Wycherley, Vanbrugh, and Congreve in the seventeenth century and Goldsmith and Sheridan in the eighteenth.

Between the two eras intervenes the comedy of the first third of the eighteenth century, the plays of Farquhar, Cibber, Steele, and Gay. These plays enjoyed a continuing popularity and presumably a continuing influence on the later dramatists. It is not fanciful to see a kinship between the genial relish for the eccentricities of rural characters in *The Beaux' Stratagem* and *She Stoops to Conquer*; between the sudden repentances of Cibber's characters and those of reprobates in mid-century comedy; between the music and love intrigue of *The Beggar's Opera* and those of *The Duenna*. *The Conscious Lovers* held the stage throughout the Garrick era (though its popularity had begun to wane in the decade before *The Rivals*),[19] and as Shirley Kenny has demonstrated it remained influential in shaping comedies written by other men: in popularizing heroines more remarkable for virtue than for wit; and heroes who, like Myrtle in Steele's play, are 'errant but fundamentally meritorious'.[20] Such heroines and heroes are easy to find in mid-eighteenth-century comedy: in *The Good Natured Man*, *The Fashionable Lover*, *The West Indian*, and even in *The Rivals* and *The School for Scandal*. Maria is scarcely a 'distressed virgin' in the mould of Steele's Indiana, but her virtue is more conspicuous than her wit; Charles Surface is indeed 'errant but fundamentally meritorious'. Yet apart from *The Conscious Lovers* and perhaps *The West Indian*, the most popular comedies of the Georgian era are scarcely 'sentimental' except in a generalized sense that is applicable to Sheridan's comedies as well. They take a genial and optimistic view of the human condition and they avoid disturbing issues. Yet they succeed by their liveliness and humour.

In comparison with Restoration comedy, Georgian comedy is bland. Theatrical monopoly and censorship alike reinforced a blandness that may be the most conspicuous liability of the comedies. Dramatists only occasionally and implicitly touch the deeper social and political concerns of the time. The record of English life preserved in Georgian drama is selective in the extreme. The beginning of what we are accustomed to call the Industrial Revolution is by tradition associated with the accession of George III in 1760. Yet the mid-century dramatists largely ignore the social dislocations that accompanied it. Theirs was a view of England limited to the preoccupations of their audience, for the most part an affluent audience that resided, part of the year at least, in London; and they were disinclined to concern themselves with the sufferings of persons of lower rank. The distressed heroines of Georgian comedy may be poor, but they are rarely below the rank of the gentry.

The dramatists were as silent about political controversy as about economic deprivation. Knowing that all plays had to be submitted in advance to the office of the Licenser, dramatists were rarely so imprudent as to write about, or even to allude to, the issues with which Parliament was preoccupied: the 'personal rule' of the King, the constitutional problems posed by John Wilkes, the attempts at reform of the electorate, English policy in India, the Regency crisis. Allusions to England's foreign wars were not totally excluded, but they are predictable in their bias: with a few exceptions, including Sheridan's *The Critic*, loyal to the Government. Sympathy for the French Revolution expressed in drama in 1790 and 1791, for example, changed abruptly to hostility in 1792 and 1793 in response to changes in the Government's policy, which led early in 1793 to war with France.[21]

Sheridan's career reveals in epitome the calculated separation of the great world of revolutionary events from the private or domestic concerns of the Georgian theatre. 'How the Play is alter'd I know not', he wrote about a planned revival of *Richard II* in 1815, '—but I find a number of passages in it, which if not *judiciously moderated*, are open to application which may produce the most inflammatory effect on the audience at this *peculiar* and perilous Crisis. . . . Beware, and listen to the wise. Keep politics out of the Theatre.'[22] This from a man writing at the end of a career that had brought not only triumphs unequalled in the drama of his time but also political prominence unequalled by any other major man of letters in the eighteenth century. In a speech in the House of Commons, 3 December 1795, he had spoken in a similar vein. 'For his own part', he is reported to have said,

> he deemed a theatre no fit place for politics, nor would he think much of the principles or taste of the man who should wish to introduce them into stage representation. With respect to the London stage, the fact however was, that the players were considered as the king's servants, and the theatre the king's theatre; and there was nothing so natural as that no pieces should be permitted that were not agreeable to His Majesty.[23]

On at least two occasions, in *The Critic* of 1779 and *Pizarro* of 1799, he did not follow his own advice—though he took care to include in both a pledge of loyalty to King and country. But in the early comedies which had made him famous, *The Rivals* and *The School for Scandal*, both of which appeared during the American Revolution, he wrote about the self-contained and seemingly secure world of the English gentry. The newspaper reviews of his early plays appear amidst alarming reports of what was happening in America. But except in cautious innuendo in *The Critic*, no hint of those events appears in his early plays—nor in those of the other important dramatists of the 1770s.

The exclusion of political issues from drama led to a concentration on personal and domestic concerns. This was not necessarily a liability. Much of the best drama ever written is private rather than public in subject. But in the Georgian theatre severe inhibitions impeded even the portrayal of personal relations. Comedy then as nearly always took the relations between the sexes as its primary subject—but with the difference that the custom of the stage impeded an exploration of the vagaries of sexual passion.[24] The audience's sense of decorum provided an effective censorship. Garrick's reworking of Wycherley's *The Country Wife* and Sheridan's of Vanbrugh's *The Relapse* seem to have been conditioned by the dramatists' knowledge of the limitations imposed by the taste of their audience rather than by concern about the Stage Licenser. 'Now, egad, I think the worst alteration is in the nicety of the audience—', complains Mr. Dangle in *The Critic* (I.i), 'No double-entendre, no smart innuendo admitted; even Vanbrugh and Congreve obliged to undergo a bungling reformation!' The stage reformers had prevailed. What we are accustomed to call 'Victorian' prudery was a fact of theatrical life for a long time before Queen Victoria was born.

Libidinous characters are not absent from Georgian comedy, but when they appear they are frequently villains, sometimes villains who repent. There was nothing new in the veneration of female chastity. Even Etherege's and Dryden's heroines are chaste in deed if not always in speech. But there is innovation in the depiction of the sexual behaviour of men. The predatory male has not disappeared from comedy, but he has undergone a change. The carefree and self-confident libertine, seeking variety of sexual gratification, only occasionally appears as an amiable figure. If we need not assume that the young heroes are virginal, we can note that their sexual adventures are implicitly censured.

Conversation about sexual relations is guarded, to the exclusion of the analytical honesty in which the Restoration dramatists excelled.

The reluctance of the dramatists to undertake the analysis of sexual passion may be seen in the plays of Goldsmith. In both his comedies a defect of personality in the principal male character produces complications of plot, and the defect in each case is fundamentally the same: a radical lack of self-confidence which inhibits a normal masculine assertiveness in courtship. Honeywood, the title character of *The Good Natured Man*, may suffer from an uncritical acceptance of the philosophy of benevolence, but there can be little doubt that his deeper problem is a lack of self-esteem. Despite the most obvious encouragement from Miss Richland, an heiress whom he loves, he cannot assume the role of an aggressive male because he is convinced that he is unworthy of her. His sexual passion can find expression only in romantic fantasy. Young Marlowe in *She Stoops to Conquer* has similar inhibitions, ones that are not uncommon in our own century. Because of timidity arising from an inadequate sense of his own worth, he cannot assume the normal role in courting a girl who is his social equal; and because his sexual passion will not be denied, he finds compensation in the pursuit of bar maids. All is put right in both plays, but only through the intervention of fortunate circumstance, aided by the resourcefulness of the young women who are compelled to assume the assertive role which the young men have foregone.

Goldsmith's treatment of his sexual themes can help us to understand the geniality—or blandness—of Georgian comedy. Goldsmith depicts a psychological affliction that is shared by many men; but rather than examining it, he uses it as a source of merriment. He scarcely confronts its sexual dimension, concentrating rather on its potential for complicating his plots. Although he isolates an important psychological subject, one that had rarely been used in Restoration and eighteenth-century comedy, he regards it merely as an amusing quirk.

In all this he was a dramatist of his time. He could not, of course, have the understanding of the sexual bases of behaviour that came with Freud. But he wrote a century after Dryden, who had examined the varieties of sexual affection with a precision and authority that have scarcely been equalled in the comedy of our own century. Even if Goldsmith had been inclined to write in the vein of *Marriage A-la-Mode*, the decorums of the theatre, if not the Stage Licenser as well, would have prevented him. Like Sheridan, who in *The Critic* described the restraints under which he worked, Goldsmith was limited by the Georgian tradition.

In its social orientation, comedy remains remarkably constant. Georgian like Restoration comedy is the preserve of the fashionable: of the gentry, the squirearchy, and the lesser nobility. Some changes there are. Dramatists may be less reluctant to introduce lords into comedy, but even so not many of them appear. The topmost reaches of society were still tacitly regarded as out of bounds. The most noticeable difference in the social world of comedy appears in the attitudes toward businessmen. The Restoration 'cit' is a vanished species in Georgian comedy, in which rich merchants, with assured places in fashionable society, often figure as the generous protectors or patrons of the young lovers. Mr. Freeport in Colman's *The English Merchant*, to name but one of many such characters, offers aid to the distressed heroine Amelia and obtains a Royal pardon for her father, a knight who had been implicated in the Rebellion of 1745. The pugnacious and defensive tone that animated Steele's defence of the social pretentions of businessmen has vanished.

This is not to say that tensions between social classes are no longer depicted. I have already referred to Cumberland's *The Fashionable Lover*, in which an unscrupulous and ambitious merchant attempts unsuccessfully to marry his daughter to a lord—in this instance, a snobbish and unscrupulous one. Between the avarice and even dishonesty of the merchant, Mr. Bridgemore, and the depravity of Lord Abberville, there is little to choose. But it is worth noting that another merchant, Mr. Aubrey, the father of the heroine, would seem to speak for the dramatist when he reproaches Bridgemore in a sententious curtain speech (V): 'learn of your fraternity a more honourable practice; and let integrity for ever remain the inseparable characteristic of an English merchant'.

Colman and Garrick's *The Clandestine Marriage*, one of the best as well as most popular of the plays, repays attention for the clarity with which it illuminates the social world of Georgian drama. The play is a comedy of manners in which characters function as satirical representatives of social and occupational groups. The troubled affairs of the young couple whose marriage is 'clandestine', if not of secondary importance in the plot, are at least secondary in interest to the tensions which emerge between a vain and fatuous lord and the family of a rich merchant, to whose elder daughter the nephew of the lord is engaged to be married. Lord Ogleby and his colourless nephew, Melville, come to Mr. Sterling's country estate with the intention of signing a marriage contract between Melville and Miss Sterling, for whom her father is to provide the enormous dowry of £80,000. But Melville finds the younger daughter Fanny more attractive, and not knowing that she is secretly married to Lovewell, an impecunious relation of Lord Ogleby, offers to accept her with a dowry of £30,000 less. In her dismay at learning of Melville's interest in her, Fanny turns for help to Lord Ogleby—but before she can explain her predicament, the foolish lord thinks she is attracted to himself, and responds delightedly. Only when the assembled company discovers Lovewell in his wife's bedchamber—in a well-contrived scene that begins in mystery which is only gradually dispelled—is the acute embarrassment of Fanny relieved.

There is a certain poignance in Fanny's distresses, but she, the lawful wife of an honourable man, is not a pathetic heroine, nor do her matrimonial problems divert attention from the social antagonisms that dominate the play. Colman and Garrick, unlike the Restoration dramatists, are impartial in their satirical attention to the two social groups. Early in the first act, Lovewell explains to his wife her father's motives: 'Money (you will excuse my frankness) is the spring of all his actions, which nothing but the idea of acquiring nobility or magnificence can ever make him forego—and these he thinks his money will purchase.' Fanny's rich aunt, Lovewell adds, has a 'contempt for every thing that does not relish of what she calls Quality'—a characterization confirmed in what follows. Later in the same act, Sterling boasts of his wealth to Lovewell: 'We'll shew you fellows at the other end of the town', Sterling says, referring to Lord Ogleby's and Melville's visit, 'how we live in the city—They shall eat gold—and drink gold—and lie in gold—'. But his brash ambition is scarcely more objectionable than Lord Ogleby's effeminate snobbery. 'That vulgar fellow Sterling,' he says to his attendants (II), 'with his city politeness, would force me down his slope last night to see a clay-colour'd ditch, which he calls a canal; and what with the dew, and the east-wind, my hips and shoulders are absolutely screw'd to my body.' His own estate is deeply encumbered, we learn (II), and a large portion of Miss Sterling's dowry is intended to repay his debts. An insight into the times is provided by Lovewell's remark to Mr. Sterling, in urging his suit for Fanny (I), that he hopes 'by diligence' to increase his own modest fortune. It is difficult indeed to encounter a gentleman in Restoration comedy who alludes to the possibility of making money.

Colman and Garrick are emphatic in their satirical depiction of the new wealth generated by commerce. Other dramatists, including Sheridan, take the new wealth for granted. A rich uncle could be brought home from India, as in *The School for Scandal*, to solve a family's problems. There is in fact a certain irony, in view of Sheridan's arraignment of Warren Hastings a decade later, in his acceptance of the dramatic convention of Indian gold as a remedy for the poverty of a deserving youth.

Sheridan's triumphs of 1775 in *The Rivals* and *The Duenna* led to Garrick's choice of him the following year as his successor in the management of Drury Lane. Without Garrick's active encouragement, Sheridan could scarcely have brought about, even with the assistance of his partners, the transactions involving very large sums of money that enabled him to emerge at the age of twenty-five as one of the proprietors of Drury Lane. Sheridan's role in the theatre was to be very unlike Garrick's, strikingly so after his election to Parliament in 1780; but in 1776 a new theatrical era had come.

As is well known, the mid-century is more remarkable for revivals of old plays and for distinguished performances by good actors than for the production of new plays of literary merit. Few but specialists in the drama now read any plays (except Goldsmith's) first produced between the Licensing Act of 1737 and *The Rivals* of 1775. This is in part owing to the inaccessibility of editions of Georgian plays. More good comedies were written during those years than we commonly assume. Yet there is no denying that mid-eighteenth-century drama, in comparison with Restoration and early-eighteenth-century drama, is undistinguished. One of the reasons why that is so may be traced to the nature of the theatres.

Walpole's Stage Licensing Act of 1737 had included two principal provisions, both of them arising from the theatrical activities of the preceding decade, when the number of theatres had been enlarged and when, following the lead of Gay in *The Beggar's Opera*, dramatists had grown progressively more audacious in their satirical assaults on the Government. Insofar as any single individual provoked the repressive legislation, it was Henry Fielding, whose Little Theatre in the Haymarket produced a group of burlesques taking Walpole and other leading political figures as their targets. Against a background of such theatrical irritants, the Licensing Act required that all new plays, and

D

all revisions of old plays, be submitted in advance for review by a stage licenser; and it prohibited the performance of plays during the winter season in theatres other than the two which held royal patents, Drury Lane and Covent Garden. The former of the provisions evoked the more frequent and the more eloquent protests; the latter may have been equally damaging to the subsequent development of drama. In any event, an effort to differentiate firmly between the consequences of the two provisions of the Act would be misleading. If official censorship kept sharp political satire out of the drama, we can assume that theatrical managers at Drury Lane and Covent Garden, who enjoyed the enormous advantage of theatrical monopoly, would not have been receptive to audacious plays. The proprietors of the two theatres shared the concern of affluent men to preserve chartered institutions. It is no accident that almost the only cutting satire directed at individuals and institutions in mid-eighteenth-century drama appears in the work of Samuel Foote, who at first by subterfuge and later by royal favour managed to circumvent the prohibitions against dramatic performances in theatres other than the patent houses.

The limitation in the number of theatres made the proprietors of Drury Lane and Covent Garden dictators in earnest of the London stage, and at least one of them, John Rich of Covent Garden, was grossly unfit for the responsibility. Several clever entrepreneurs, of whom Foote was the most accomplished, found expedients for evading the theatrical monopoly; but the monopoly was with minor exceptions enforced, with the result that an aspiring dramatist had only two good markets for his wares.

Nor was either market very receptive to new plays—for a comprehensible financial reason. Old plays were proven commodities, and they could be performed without the expense of authors' benefit nights. London was large, and so was the proportion of it who wished to attend the theatre.[25] With audiences that had no alternatives to the patent houses if they wished to see plays, the managers could do as they wished in establishing their repertories; and they did not often wish to give an opportunity to a new dramatist.

To be sure, Garrick's record at Drury Lane was better than his competitors' at Covent Garden. A modern study demonstrates in statistical detail differences in the theatres' managerial policies. Drury Lane under Garrick, G. W. Stone writes, 'produced 63 new mainpieces and 107 new afterpieces, for an average of 2 and nearly 4 respectively each year'. During the same period, Mr. Stone explains, Covent Garden 'produced 51 new mainpieces and 47 new afterpieces, for an average of one and a half respectively each year'.[26] Drury Lane had a better record than Covent Garden but still, if we look at the number of new plays, not a very good record. We can understand why men of letters such as Oliver Goldsmith were dissatisfied.

In his *Enquiry into the Present State of Polite Learning in Europe*, Goldsmith writes caustically about the theatres—so caustically, that he seems to have offended Garrick.[27] Goldsmith writes with the bias of a man of letters, revealing the perennial author's resentment of the predominance in the theatres of managers and actors. Much of what he says is anticipated in John Dennis's writings during Queen Anne's and George I's reigns, though Goldsmith justly asserts that the status of the actor had risen in the intervening years. 'In the times of Addison and Steele, players were held in greater contempt than, perhaps, they deserved. Honest Eastcourt, Verbruggen and Underhill, were extremely poor, and assumed no airs of insolence.' True, but Goldsmith chooses to ignore the more prosperous actors of that time, Robert Wilks, Barton Booth, and Colley Cibber, whose affluence and social prominence evoked criticism scarcely different from that Goldsmith levels at the mid-century actors. Yet conditions had changed. Goldsmith describes the barriers facing the dramatists of his own time:

> From the nature therefore of our theatre, and the genius of our country, it is extremely difficult for a dramatic poet to please his audience. But happy would he be were these the only difficulties he had to encounter; there are many other more dangerous combinations against the little wit of the age. Our poet's performance must undergo a process truly chymical before it is presented to the public. It must be tried in the manager's fire, strained through a licenser, and purified in the Review or the news-paper of the day.

Goldsmith writes realistically about the managers' preference for revivals of old plays over the performance of new ones: 'I AM not insensible that third nights are disagreeable drawbacks upon the annual profits of the stage; I am confident, it is much more to the manager's advantage to furbish up all the lumber which the good sense of our ancestors, but for his care, had consign'd to oblivion.' Goldsmith's comment on the delay an author experienced helps to explain why so few new plays were performed: 'I HAVE been informed, that no new play can be admitted upon our theatre unless the author chuses to wait some years, or to use the phrase in fashion, till it comes to be played in turn'. He regrets the prominence of scene design and of interludes of dancing in the theatres. He protests what he regards as the reversal of the just relationship between the play and the actor who performs in it: 'No matter what the play may be, it is the actor who draws an audience.'

The chapter '*Of the STAGE*' is caustic and it leaves much unsaid, but it is not an inaccurate account of conditions in the theatre which discouraged dramatists or potential dramatists. Yet Goldsmith neglects to acknowledge the quality of entertainment offered the theatres' patrons. Reading a calender of performances in the Garrick era can make a modern play-goer—though not a modern playwright—envious. Owing to the researches of Mr. Stone,[28] we know the offerings of Drury Lane and Covent Garden in precise detail, and we can but wonder nostalgically at the number and variety of good plays performed, often very well performed. At Drury Lane in the years from 1747 to 1776 there was a total of 492 performances of Shakespeare's tragedies, with an average of seventeen each season. The ten most popular tragedies during these years included four of Shakespeare's and included as well Congreve's *The Mourning Bride*, Otway's *The Orphan* and *Venice Preserved*, Rowe's *The Fair Penitent* and *Jane Shore*, and Aaron Hill's *Zara*, an adaption of Voltaire's *Zaire*. Covent Garden's record in tragedy is not very different, with Shakespeare again far ahead of all rivals, but with Lee and Rowe prominently represented.

The repertories in comedy of the two theatres have more relevance to Sheridan's career, and will repay a closer look. In both instances, mid-eighteenth-century plays appear among those most frequently performed, though they remain collectively far less prominent than the older plays. At the top of the list for Drury Lane is Benjamin Hoadly's *The Suspicious Husband*, though the fact that it was first produced (at Covent Garden) in 1747 gives it a statistical advantage over plays that came later in the twenty-year period covered by Stone's figures. Cumberland's *The West Indian* of 1771, for example, achieved in five years approximately half as many performances as *The Suspicious Husband* in four times as many seasons. Apart from these two plays, among the fifteen most frequently performed at Drury Lane, appear Colman and Garrick's *The Clandestine Marriage*, Colman's *The Jealous Wife*, and Murphy's *The Way to Keep Him*. Although the group includes three of Shakespeare's and two of Jonson's, it includes only one late-seventeenth-century comedy, Vanbrugh's *The Provoked Wife* —a circumstance that accentuates the importance of Sheridan's Restoration revivals and adaptations after 1776. Yet four early-eighteenth-century comedies appear among the most popular at Drury Lane: *The Beaux' Stratagem*, *The Conscious Lovers*, *The Provoked Husband*, and *The Wonder*.

At Covent Garden the most frequently performed comedies reveal a similar heterogeneity and a similar pattern, except that only one mid-eighteenth-century play, Hoadly's *The Suspicious Husband*, is among the most popular. Again Shakespeare and Jonson alone among the Renaissance dramatists are represented, and again early-eighteenth-century comedy is more strongly represented than late-seventeenth. Except for *The Suspicious Husband*, the most popular comedies at Covent Garden as well as at Drury Lane were written in the early years of the eighteenth century: *The Provoked Husband*, *The Beaux' Stratagem*, and *The Conscious Lovers*. More was involved in the lack of popularity of mid-eighteenth-century comedy than governmental control of the theatres, but these records of performances will suggest, though they cannot prove, that the Licensing Act of 1737 which enforced theatrical monopoly and thereby limited the possibilities for the performance of new plays was indeed damaging to Georgian drama.

3

Restoration Comedy in Georgian Burlesque, *The Rivals* and *The Duenna*

Even before the first performance of *The School for Scandal*, Samuel Johnson proposed Sheridan for membership in The Club. 'He who has written the two best comedies of the age,' Johnson said, referring to *The Rivals* and *The Duenna*, 'is surely a considerable man.'[1] However considerable, he was not yet twenty-six years old; when his final important play, *The Critic*, was produced in 1779, he was still only twenty-eight. He was precocious and prolific; we are reminded of Congreve by his age when his plays were first performed as by much else in his career.

'The two best comedies of the age'—high praise, too high in the opinion of many; and furthermore, in Johnson's use of the superlative, conveying criticism of other Georgian comedies. Yet the opinion was defensible at the time Johnson spoke, and it is close enough to an accurate appraisal to merit attention. We are disinclined to take the praise of *The Duenna* seriously. But let us remember that it is a comic opera which we have never seen and heard in performance. Certainly it held the stage for a long time. William Hazlitt, who had seen and heard it, approximates Johnson's evaluation of it:

> The Duenna is a perfect work of art. It has the utmost sweetness and point. The plot, the characters, the dialogue, are all complete in themselves, and they are all his own; and the songs are the best that ever were written, except those in the Beggar's Opera.[2]

All of Sheridan's plays are more impressive to a spectator than to a reader, but the difference in impact made by *The Rivals*, *The School for Scandal*, and *The Critic* is by no means so considerable as in the two musical plays, *The Duenna* and *Pizarro*. Johnson's high praise of *The Rivals* is comprehensible to us because we can see it on stage, acted by professional as well as amateur companies. When we have before us the living presence of skilled actors and actresses who can give visual reinforcement to the incongruities of situation and language conveyed by Sheridan's dialogue,[3] we are likely to be insensitive to faults we discover in a close reading of the text.

The Rivals and *The Duenna* are separated by only a short interval of time, from January until November 1775; and despite the obvious differences separating the comedy from the opera they have much in common. In both of them Sheridan played variations on dramatic formulae of the Restoration that had survived into the eighteenth century. In its plot of Spanish intrigue, *The Duenna* may be even closer than *The Rivals* to Restoration precedent, in this instance to the sub-genre established by Sir Samuel Tuke, the Earl of Bristol, and Dryden, among others, which Dryden called the 'Spanish plot.' Sheridan was a young man in a hurry, a young man of genius and of enormous energy and inventiveness, but one who took promising dramatic materials where he could find them, reworking them in his own idiom, which for all his Restoration borrowings was a Georgian idiom. If he imitated dramatists of the preceding century, he did so in his first two plays in a spirit of burlesque, repeating theatrical clichés but doing so with such audacity and ingenuity of execution that the conventionality, far from being a liability, becomes in its allusiveness a source of delight.

In *The Rivals* scarcely less than in *The Duenna* the humour is primarily situational, arising from incongruous confrontations that come about when one or more of the characters does not know the identity of one or more of the others. Captain Jack Absolute's assuming the name and and rank of Ensign Beverley results in almost as many misunderstand-ings and comical confrontations as arise when Clara and Louisa are mistaken for one another. In both the play and the opera the tyrannical attempt of the older generation to direct the affairs of the younger precipitates the defensive stratagems of the young lovers on which the two plots move. The dialogue of neither *The Rivals* nor *The Duenna* approximates the sustained brilliance of that of *The School for Scandal*, in which even casual conversation frequently reaches to epigram, but in both the earlier works witty remarks—whether intended by the dramatic characters speaking them or not—come steadily. And at least in *The Rivals* the dialogue sometimes rises to striking effect, as in the contrast established between the diction of Sir Anthony and that of Mrs. Malaprop. Sheridan's haste in writing *The Rivals* and *The Duenna* resulted in dialogue that approximates more closely to unrehearsed conversation than that in *The School for Scandal*—and in the first act of *The Critic*—and it may have forced him to rely more consistently on situational humour. But there were compensating gains in rapidity of movement and in the seeming spontaneity of the characters' actions.

Both *The Rivals* and *The Duenna* are in a restricted and specialized sense 'family plays'—that is to say, plays in which there are subdued and disguised recollections of Sheridan's and his wife's recent experiences and also plays in which he drew on the writings or the skills of members of his own or his wife's family. Neither *The Rivals* nor *The Duenna* is autobiographical. That is beyond dispute. Yet there are references in innuendo to recent events that Sheridan's first audiences would have recognized. To give one example cited by his niece, Alicia Lefanu, 'The ridiculous and contradictory reports then afloat [after Sheridan's duels with Thomas Mathews], certainly give rise to the highly humourous duel scenes in "The Rivals" and "The School for Scandal".'[4] (In the reference to the latter play, Alicia Lefanu presumably alludes to the baseless gossip about a duel in Act V, scene ii.) Other aspects of *The Rivals* may be interpreted as a comic commentary on the romantic history of Elizabeth Linley and Sheridan's courtship of her. So too with *The Duenna*. The author of the most detailed biography of Sheridan, Walter Sichel, remarks that Sheridan's elopement with Elizabeth 'haunts the measures of "The Duenna" '.[5] I must consider all this later. At the moment it is enough to say that, like almost every other young writer, Sheridan made capital of his own experience.

He made capital as well of the musical talents of the family into which he had married and, to a lesser extent, of the fragment of a comedy by his mother, left incomplete at her death. Even without surviving letters that corroborate the fact, we could assume that there was a connection between *The Duenna* and his marriage two years before it was first performed to a famous singer who was the daughter of a composer. The Linleys had a major part in the preparation of *The Duenna* for the stage. On the other hand, his deceased mother's part in

The Rivals was limited to ideas and phrases he could take over from her uncompleted comedy, *A Journey to Bath*.[6] He took little—little, that is, if we are to judge from his play without knowledge of the stages of his writing and revising it before the submission of his manuscript to the Stage Licenser.

For all their proximity in time and their resemblances to one another, *The Rivals* and *The Duenna* provide respectively examples of two distinct forms of drama, 'comedy of character' on the one hand, and 'comedy of action' on the other. The plot of the earlier play, though intricate and well contrived, is subordinate to the display of the whims and humours of the characters; the plot of the opera is primary, most of the characters serving merely as counters in the elaboration of the intrigues. In *The Duenna* Sheridan follows Spanish precedent in giving priority to plot over characterization, a fact the more striking because in *The Rivals* the plot, secondary in interest, is a vehicle manipulated to reveal the idiosyncrasies of the characters. The gallery of eccentric characters in *The Rivals* is recognizably in a tradition that can be traced to Ben Jonson. In *The Duenna*, on the other hand, only one character, Isaac Mendoza, is sharply individualized. Three of the lovers are, as to personal traits, interchangeable with many others in English adaptations and imitations of the Spanish *comedia*. The fourth, Ferdinand, intermittently and in milder form displays something of the self-tormenting jealousy that is so prominent in Faulkland of *The Rivals*. But of Clara and Louisa one could say what a hostile critic once said of the heroines of Calderón's cape and sword plays, that they are as much alike as cannon balls. Louisa's father, Don Jerome, responds just as we would expect a suspicious father to do, though he shows more concern for money than for family honour. (It is typical of the *comedia* that a father rather than a mother represents the older generation.) The duenna is grotesque enough in appearance, but again little is made of her personal qualities. Only Isaac Mendoza, the opportunistic convert to Christianity, is clearly an eccentric, a fop in whom greed conquers all—even his aversion to the elderly duenna. Sheridan had his eye firmly fixed on the misunderstandings which propel his plot.

Like many another seventeenth- and eighteenth-century comedy, *The Rivals* has a plot that turns on love and money, and specifically on conflicting attitudes held by the young as well as by their more prudent elders about the relative importance of those components of marriage settlements. The willingness of both Lydia and Julia to marry a man for love whom they mistakenly assume has no fortune represents a financial disinterest for which it would be difficult to find a parallel in Restoration comedy. Yet Sheridan does not put the young couples to the test but rather, like nearly every other dramatist of his century, evades the reality of poverty by ensuring his young lovers of the needed wealth. He was writing comedy, and he was content to accept the prosperous denouement of theatrical convention.

His burlesque of the tyranny of the older generation in the persons of Sir Anthony and Mrs. Malaprop should not conceal the force of the social reality which lay behind that tyranny—the custom among affluent families of arranging marriages with close attention to property settlements.[7] Sheridan wrote in the interval between Richardson's *Clarissa* and Jane Austen's *Pride and Prejudice*. A state of affairs that in Richardson leads to tragedy and in Jane Austen to poignant humiliation provides Sheridan with a subject for burlesque. 'Odd's life, Sir!', Sir Anthony exclaims to Jack (II.i), 'if you have the estate, you must take it with the live stock on it, as it stands.' This is a familiar parental attitude in Restoration comedy, and some of the seventeenth-century fathers—Sir Sampson Legend of Congreve's *Love for Love*, for example—are scarcely less 'absolute' in their decisions than Sir Anthony. Yet it would be hard to find in Etherege, Wycherley, Congreve, or Vanbrugh the sustained ridicule of tyranny that accompanies Sheridan's depiction of Sir Anthony and Mrs. Malaprop. Sheridan refuses to take the old conventions of plot and character as more than a source for ridiculous situations.

His burlesque of parental tyranny notwithstanding, Sheridan has limited tolerance for financially imprudent marriages. His authorial judgements—in *The Rivals* we have little difficulty in determining where his own sympathies lie—reveal a reverence for English social institutions as marked as that of Henry Fielding, whose opinion on financial settlements in marriage would seem to be articulated by his title character in *Don Quixote in England* (III): 'Money is a Thing well worth considering in these Affairs;' says the Spanish knight with eminent good sense, 'but Parents always regard it too much, and Lovers too little.' Only one of Sheridan's characters, Lydia, regards it 'too little', though Julia professes a willingness to accept Faulkland even when he falsely claims to have lost everything as a consequence of an imaginary duel. Sheridan's is the affluent world of social and financial practicality familiar in Restoration and eighteenth-century comedy, in which a rich and repulsive suitor such as Bob Acres might be rejected in favour of a rich and attractive suitor such as Jack Absolute, but in which misalliances do not occur except as a form of punishment, outside the absurd fantasies of a girl whose head has been turned by reading novels.

Parental tyranny exercised in the choice of a spouse for a son, daughter, or ward, that principal subject of *The Rivals* as of many Restoration comedies, may well have been enacted in cruel reality in the Linley family. Referring to the letters which record the vagaries of fortune to which the three Linley sisters were subjected, George Saintsbury aptly remarked that they 'fit on in a curious comparison-contrast way to Miss Austen's prosopopaeia'.[8] At the age of sixteen Elizabeth, already celebrated as a singer and a beauty, had been betrothed by her parents to an elderly but wealthy man. Sir Anthony Absolute shows far more concern for the happiness of his son than Thomas Linley did for the happiness of his daughter—to the twentieth-century mind, at least—when for no discernible reason except a financial one he entered into a formal contract of betrothal, on behalf of Elizabeth, with Walter Long, described by those who wrote about the strange episode as aged sixty.[9] To be sure, Thomas Linley and his wife would have understood from personal experience the advantages that wealth brought. Their motives may not have been entirely selfish. Precisely why the engagement was broken off, with Walter Long making Elizabeth a handsome settlement of three thousand pounds as compensation for the humiliation she had suffered, as well as for the loss sustained in her earnings as a singer, is not fully understood.[10] Yet the episode would suggest that the parental tyranny so bluntly satirized in *The Rivals* was no phantom in the world Sheridan had known. If in the genial atmosphere of the imaginary world of earlier Georgian comedy, parents who exploit their children appear less frequently than in the comedy of a hundred years before, the historical reality that was the satirist's target had changed less than the literary record might suggest.

We have no reason to assume that Sheridan's emphasis in *The Rivals* on the antagonism between the generations derived from his wife's bitter experiences. That antagonism had long been traditional in comedy, as Sheridan must have known despite his insistence in the preface on the originality of his play. His limited knowledge of earlier drama, he writes, led him into many errors:

> Yet I own that, in one respect, I did not regret my ignorance:
> for as my first wish in attempting a Play, was to avoid every
> appearance of plagiary, I thought I should stand a better chance
> of effecting this from being in a walk which I had not frequented,
> and where consequently the progress of invention was less likely
> to be interrupted by starts of recollection: for on subjects on
> which the mind has been much informed, invention is slow of
> exerting itself.

We need not doubt that Sheridan believed what he said, nor that
The Rivals is indeed 'original'—but, as Sheridan put it in his preface,
'Faded ideas float in the fancy like half-forgotten dreams,' and writers
may unknowingly take suggestions from their predecessors.[11]

In any event, *The Rivals* even more than *The School for Scandal*
resembles earlier plays, Congreve's among others, in character types,
relationships between characters, and complications of plot. *The Rivals*
is very different from *The School for Scandal*: less subtle, less cynical,
and more derivative from comic tradition. It may not be fanciful to see
a parallel relationship between the first and last full-length comedies
of Congreve and Sheridan. To encounter Fainall and Mrs. Marwood in
The Way of the World after reading *The Old Bachelor* is to encounter
the more painful awareness of malignancy that differentiates *The School
for Scandal* from *The Rivals*. Although Sheridan was a young man who
could have had only a limited experience of the London theatres, he
belonged to a theatrical family. He could scarcely have been so ignorant
of earlier drama as he implies in the preface to *The Rivals*. He had no
need of a literary historian's knowledge to be familiar with such
conventional motifs as antagonism between the generations arising
from conflicting conceptions of the importance of love and money in
marriage settlements.

His Lydia Languish, like Congreve's Millamant of *The Way of the
World*, will lose a large portion of her fortune if she marries without
the permission of her aunt: a loss of two-thirds for Lydia, of one-half
for Millamant. Lydia's romantic indifference to money notwithstanding, young Jack Absolute is as prudentially calculating in financial
affairs as Mirabel; and like Mirabel he finds himself compelled to
ingratiate himself with the aunt—no easy task when Mrs. Malaprop
discovers that he is the author of letters unflattering to herself. Mrs.
Malaprop is not immune to love despite the shadow of her years,

and, in her susceptibility to the unintended overtures of Sir Lucius O'Trigger, she is, like Lady Wishfort when she discovers Sir Rowland to be an impostor, at once absurd and pathetic. Mirabel is not provided with a father, but Valentine in *Love for Love* has just such a headstrong and warm-blooded father as Sir Anthony Absolute, one who is even more envious of his son's prospects of erotic delight than Sir Anthony. Jack Absolute's father stops short of Sir Sampson Legend's rivalry with his son for the girl, but he cannot withhold an unfatherly expression of admiration for her (III.i): 'Odds life! I've a great mind to marry the girl myself!'

The resemblances of *The Rivals* to Congreve's comedies, as to other seventeenth-century comedies, are of the generalized kind that derive from a shared literary tradition. A more specific anticipation of an important aspect of *The Rivals* appears in George Colman's *Polly Honeycombe*, an afterpiece first produced in 1760. Sheridan, it has been noted,[12] might have seen a revival of it in February 1773, a time when he may have been in London. Colman's title character, like Lydia Languish, has had her head turned by over much reading of prose fiction. Yet Colman as well as Sheridan drew on a satirical tradition as old as Cervantes's *Don Quixote*; we cannot feel assurance that Sheridan drew on Colman rather than the shared tradition, of which several other English works of the eighteenth century including Steele's *The Tender Husband* of 1705 are expressions.[13] Still, Lydia Languish is so remarkably like Polly Honeycombe that recollections of the earlier character might have floated in Sheridan's 'fancy like half-forgotten dreams'.

Colman called his short play 'A Dramatic Novel', a descriptive phrase that is appropriate at least in the sense that it suggests his primary satirical target, one not different in kind from that of Cervantes or, to cite an example from Georgian England, that of Charlotte Lennox in her novel *The Female Quixote* of 1752. Colman provides in *Polly Honeycombe* a comical and hostile critique of the mid-eighteenth-century vogue of the sentimental novel. He is in fact more hostile to 'sentimentality' than Sheridan fifteen years later in *The Rivals*. So charming a young woman as the Lydia Languish of Sheridan's play can scarcely convey a satirical admonition to an audience. Captain Absolute may be exasperated by her romantic fantasies, but not to the point where he ceases to love and court her, even at the inconvenience of assuming a false name and reduced rank. Not so with Polly

Honeycombe, whose aberration produces graver consequences. In her folly she alienates not only her fiancé, an intelligent if unimaginative young man of business, but also the suitor she prefers, a lawyer's clerk, whose affection for her does not survive a confrontation with her father. The father's final remark, 'a man might as well turn his Daughter loose in Covent-garden, as trust the cultivation of her mind to A CIRCULATING LIBRARY', suggests Colman's satirical intention.

That intention notwithstanding, the little play has, in the words of R. W. Bevis, 'a second face: while it purports to castigate the circulating library, it half sympathizes with the Pollys and ridicules their oppressors'.[14] Polly is indeed, as she insists, subject to her father's manipulation, and, like Steele's Biddy Tipkin of *The Tender Husband*, she lives in circumstances that stifle the imaginative side of her nature. We must feel some sympathy for her plight. Yet Colman refuses to permit her the happy escape that Steele and Sheridan provide for their own devotees of prose fiction. The result is a curiously bitter if psychologically convincing denouement for a semi-farcical afterpiece.

Whatever the unknowable facts about Sheridan's literary borrowings, the similarities between *Polly Honeycombe* and *The Rivals* illustrate the continuity of Georgian dramatic tradition. So also the similarities between *The Rivals* and Garrick's afterpiece of 1747, *Miss in Her Teens*, in which a climactic duel scene resembles Sheridan's and a group of characters corresponds to those in Sheridan's main plot.[15] Even Sheridan's 'neurotic lover' Faulkland, it has recently been noted, may owe something to a character in Arthur Murphy's *All in the Wrong*, 1761, Murphy having based his character on one in Fielding's *Love in Several Masques*, 1728.[16] Sheridan was using old and familiar materials. Yet by choosing to accentuate the traditional materials, he achieved an effect that is all his own.

Mrs. Malaprop provides the most remarkable instance of his reworking and exaggerating a venerable dramatic device: pomposity coupled with inexact choice of words. Julia refers with a lexicographer's precision to Mrs. Malaprop's fault of diction (I.ii.), 'her select words so ingeniously *misapplied*, without being *mispronounced*'. Shakespeare's Dogberry and many later characters, too many for it to be worth while naming them, share the fault. Yet we may plausibly assume that Sheridan took the idea for the character, as he certainly took some phrases, from his mother's Mrs. Tryfort in her unfinished comedy *A Journey to Bath*. Sheridan's father had given him the manuscript after his mother's death and he made use of it, though his completed play bears little apparent resemblance to *A Journey to Bath*.[17] In fact even while he retained and emphasized the character's habits of speech, he changed her social position and in so doing the motive which prompted her overzealous effort to achieve an elegance of diction. Mrs. Tryfort, 'a citizens widow,' is a late representative of the familiar Restoration character type of a woman with unseemly social ambition. Mrs. Malaprop, on the other hand, is a provincial gentlewoman of assured position whose fault arises from intellectual rather than social affectation. The old antagonism between citizen and gentry had long since outworn its usefulness as a subject for comedy, and Sheridan knew it. He discarded the subject, replacing it with one having contemporary relevance, the intellectual aspirations of that group of feminists we call 'blue-stockings.'[18]

Thomas Moore remarked of *The Rivals* that Sheridan 'overcharged most of his persons with whims and absurdities, for which the circumstances they are engaged in afford but a very disproportionate vent.'[19] Yet it is from this gallery of characters 'overcharged . . . with whims and absurdities' that the force of the play derives. Young Absolute and Julia alone among the principal characters lack a defining quality, an idiosyncracy akin to a Jonsonian 'humour'. The exaggerated emphasis on the foibles of the characters establishes the tone of the play, that of burlesque or a near approach to it. Several of the characters resemble well-defined types of Restoration comedy: Sir Anthony the tyrannical father, Mrs. Malaprop the would-be wit, Bob Acres the booby squire who is also a would-be wit—but they are rather burlesques of the old types than representatives of them. The play is not without a strong narrative line. Misrepresentations and misunderstandings follow hard on one another. Yet the narrative functions primarily as a means of displaying the absurdities of the characters. The barriers confronting the two couples are of their own making, deriving either from overactive imaginations or from ignorance of their tyrannical elders' intentions.

Each of the principal characters is paired with another who is conspicuous for the possession of or lack of the quality that distinguishes the complementary character: Sir Lucius O'Trigger with 'Fighting Bob Acres'; Mrs. Malaprop with Sir Anthony, whose formal and precise diction would scarcely be expected from a country squire; the sensible though romantic Julia with the neurotic Faulkland;

Lydia with Jack Absolute, who has no intention of sacrificing any part of his intended bride's dowry. Contrasts between the paired characters provide the best remembered episodes: among others, Sir Anthony's conversations with Mrs. Malaprop, and Sir Lucius's advice to Bob Acres on the field of honour. The pairings all relate to the principal love intrigue. Lydia and Jack erroneously believe that Mrs. Malaprop and Sir Anthony are opposed to their union. Sir Lucius and Bob Acres are nominally suitors for Lydia, and it is they who precipitate the duel which brings the denouement.

Sheridan is tolerant of Lydia's romantic imagination; he is less tolerant of Faulkland's, though eighteenth-century audiences and presumably Sheridan himself had more sympathy for him than we have. His neurotic musings seem to us incompatible with the happy tone of semi-farcical humour which is otherwise sustained. He is disturbing because he is a convincing portrait of a self-tormentor. Psychological authenticity has a limited place in comedy that so frequently employs burlesque as this one. Faulkland's self-inflicted sufferings provide too frequent reminders of our own vulnerability to the uncontrolled imagination. He saved Julia's life in a boating accident; her deceased father gave his blessing to their intended marriage; Julia has assured him of her love for him. Yet, he asks himself obsessively, does she indeed love him or is she prepared to accept him merely out of gratitude to him and duty to her late father?

The character had his admirers as well as his critics among the first audiences. 'Faulkland is a great proof of heart-felt delicacy'; wrote a contributor to *The Morning Chronicle*, 27 January 1775, 'he is a beautiful exotic, and tho' not found in every garden, we cannot deny it may in some; the exquisite refinement in his disposition, opposed to the noble simplicity, tenderness, and candor of Julia's, gives rise to some of the most affecting sentimental scenes I ever remember to have met with.' This is not a response to the character which would have been endorsed by all,[20] nor is it, I think, the response that Sheridan intended to evoke. Yet it will serve as a reminder that 'the age of sensibility' had not passed and that Sheridan shared with his recently deceased contemporary Laurence Sterne an affectionate regard for sensibility even while burlesquing it. *A Sentimental Journey* was less than a decade in the past. We can understand Sheridan's satirical objective, and we can also understand the function of Faulkland as a male counterpart of Lydia Languish. Julia associates Lydia's and Faulkland's afflictions when she attempts to dissuade Lydia from her capricious rejection of Jack (V.i.):

> If I were in spirits, Lydia, I should chide you only by laughing heartily at you: but it suits more the situation of my mind, at present, earnestly to entreat you, not to let a man, who loves you with sincerity, suffer that unhappiness from your *caprice*, which I know too well caprice can inflict.

Julia speaks with such good sense that we may assume she speaks for the author. Yet if Julia is clear-headed and practical, as Lydia is not, she can speak in the romantic vein of her lover. Although no self-tormentor, she has sensibility enough to understand the 'caprice' of Lydia and Faulkland.

We find Lydia's romantic fantasy entertaining, partly because it is a happy fantasy, partly because it is less inappropriate to her sex; and we find Faulkland's soliloquies only intermittently amusing. They are an expression of pain, not the less real because self-inflicted, and they seem unmanly in a play that celebrates manliness. Faulkland may appear unworthy of so spirited and sensible a girl as Julia. He possesses neither the benevolence of Goldsmith's Honeywood and young Marlow, both of whom are also victims of insufficient self-esteem, nor the assertiveness of Jack Absolute. Yet in 1775 he could be recognized as it is difficult for us to recognize him today, as a rendering of a 'man of feeling', a satirical rendering but one not critical to the exclusion of sympathy or even qualified admiration.

Faulkland's neurotic musings as well as Lydia's romantic fantasies provide Sheridan with targets in his critique of 'sentimental comedy'. He made his critique explicit in a prologue for the tenth performance of the play. 'Yet this adorn'd with every graceful art', he wrote about the personification of comedy,

> To charm the fancy and yet reach the heart—
> Must we displace her? And instead advance
> The Goddess of the woeful countenance—
> The sentimental Muse! . . .

The rhetorical question is answered as we would expect, in a complaint about the intrusion into comedy of subjects appropriate to tragedy. The prologue is a contribution to the old but continuing debate about the nature of comedy, a graceful contribution though scarcely original. Yet it is worth noting his phrase 'and yet reach the heart'—a phrase appropriate to Georgian comedy including Sheridan's own plays but

E

scarcely appropriate to the best of Restoration comedy. Sheridan neatly isolates, whether or not he intended to do so, a pervasive quality of Georgian comedy, its emotional softness, present in *The Rivals* as well as in comedies which 'advance . . . The sentimental Muse!'

In our own time Faulkland seems the least successful character, the only major character whose personality seems at once enigmatic and incongruous in the happy world of the play. Yet it was not Faulkland but Sir Lucius O'Trigger who in the first performance, 17 January 1775, before the play was withdrawn for revision, aroused the most vehement criticism. 'Sir Lucius O'Trigger', wrote a contributor to *The Morning Post*, 21 January 1775, 'was so ungenerous an attack upon a nation, that must justify any severity with which the piece will hereafter be treated: it is the first time I ever remember to have seen so villainous a portrait of an Irish Gentleman, permitted so openly to insult that country upon the boards of an English theatre.'[21] *The Morning Chronicle*, 18 January 1775, was unequivocal in its opinion both of the actor who played the role, John Lee, and of the role itself: 'What evil spirit could influence the writer and the manager to assign the part of Sir *Lucius O'Trigger* to Mr. Lee, or Lee himself to receive it?' The dramatic character received even harsher criticism than the actor who had the role: 'This representation of Sir Lucius, is indeed an affront to the common sense of an audience, and is so far from giving the manners of our brave and worthy neighbours, that it scarce equals the picture of a respectable Hotentot: . . .' Though he had the protection of his own Irish origin, Sheridan had reason enough to alter the character and to see that some other actor took the role when the play was again performed on 28 January. This time the character succeeded splendidly, though the improvement owed more to the reassignment of the role to a suitable actor, Lawrence Clinch, than to the revisions Sheridan made.[22] Sheridan cleared up some ambiguities of action and softened some phrases which could give offense, but the character remains a conventional Irishman—in the words of a modern scholar, 'the most finished and amusing stage Irishman' of the Georgian era.[23]

Before the first performance of *The Rivals*, there was understandably speculation that the play would be autobiographical. Few men of twenty-four in Sheridan's or in any other time had had such an adventurous and well-publicized courtship as he. Before Sheridan's marriage to Elizabeth Linley in 1773, he had escorted her to France so that she could escape the unwelcome attentions of a married army officer, Thomas Mathews. After returning to England, Sheridan fought two duels with Mathews, the second nearly fatal to himself. The beauty and the fame of Elizabeth as a singer, the elopement followed by the two duels, and their subsequent marriage made the Sheridans something more than an anonymous young couple even before the success of *The Rivals*. It is not fanciful to assume that the publicity to which Sheridan and his wife had been subjected eased the way for the young dramatist in gaining a hearing for his first play.

The expectations that *The Rivals* would be autobiographical were of course disappointed: Sheridan's keen sense of propriety and personal honour excluded overt allusion to his wife's misfortunes. 1775 was the year of a well-known conversation about Sheridan, reported by Boswell, which turned on the propriety of Sheridan's refusal to allow his wife to sing in public. Boswell's paragraph on the subject merits quotation in full for the insight it provides into Sheridan's state of mind in the year that brought both *The Rivals* and *The Duenna*:

> We talked of a young gentleman's marriage with an eminent singer, and his determination that she should no longer sing in publick, though his father was very earnest she should, because her talents would be liberally rewarded, so as to make her a good fortune. It was questioned whether the young gentleman, who had not a shilling in the world, but was blest with very uncommon talents, was not foolishly delicate, or foolishly proud, and his father truely rational without being mean. Johnson, with all the high spirit of a Roman senator, exclaimed, 'He resolved wisely and nobly to be sure. He is a brave man. Would not a gentleman be disgraced by having his wife singing publickly for hire? No, Sir, there can be no doubt here. I know not if I should not *prepare* myself for a publick singer, as readily as let my wife be one.'[24]

Whether Johnson was right that Sheridan would have been 'disgraced' by allowing his wife to sing in public poses a question that is scarcely answerable in the twentieth century. But we can be sure that Sheridan was a brave man—brave, proud, sensitive to affront, and keenly aware of his own and his wife's vulnerability to gossip mongers.[25] His was not merely the physical bravery evident in the duels with Mathews but also a more pervasive kind of audacity, later characteristic of his debates in Parliament, and in his youth evident in the rapidity with which he wrote and revised his plays and in the spirit with which he responded to the acerbity of newspaper critics in *The School for Scandal* and *The Critic*.

Sheridan did not dramatize his own or his wife's romantic adventures. Yet he chose Bath as the locale of *The Rivals*, he included a pugnacious Irishman among his characters, he brought the play to a climax in a comical duel scene, and he allowed characters to talk about elopement in a romantic vein that would have put a quick-witted audience in mind of his personal history. Sir Lucius O'Trigger, a proud and hot-blooded Irishman, is like Sheridan ready to win a lady with his sword. This stage Irishman, so broadly drawn before the play was revised as to have provoked angry protests, challenges Jack Absolute for no better reason than that Jack is the favoured suitor of Lydia Languish, to whom the deluded O'Trigger aspires. 'Can a man commit a more heinous offence against another,' Sir Lucius asks Bob Acres (III.iv), 'than to fall in love with the same woman?' Thomas Mathews might have said this to Sheridan. O'Trigger resembles Thomas Mathews in nothing except his pugnacity and his love for a lady who will not have him; O'Trigger resembles Sheridan himself in nothing except his pugnacity and nationality. Yet O'Trigger, like Bob Acres of Clod Hall, fancies himself the *rival* of Captain Absolute (or 'Ensign Beverley'). How could an audience fail to think of the rivals in the two recent duels, Mathews and Sheridan, who had fought for the love of a beautiful lady? Not autobiography or self-parody, the half-submerged allusions to episodes known to his audience nevertheless represent a subtle and tactful means of making capital of personal celebrity.

Nor are the tentative allusions to Sheridan's own history confined to the duellists. Both Lydia and Julia speak longingly of a romantic elopement, and many in Sheridan's audience would have known about his trip to France with Elizabeth Linley. The audience would have known, from Samuel Foote's *The Maid of Bath* if not from gossip and the newspapers as well, about Elizabeth's earlier betrothal, a financial venture on the part of her parents. 'To find myself made a mere Smithfield bargain of at last!' (V.i) exclaims Lydia, when she learns Jack's true identity. 'There had I projected one of the most sentimental elopements!—so becoming a disguise!—so amiable a ladder of Ropes!' Julia's suggestion to Faulkland, after he has falsely claimed that he must leave the kingdom, approximates more closely

Elizabeth Linley and Sheridan's experience—flight to another country
before marriage (V.i):

> My heart had long known no other guardian—I now entrust
> my person to your honour—we will fly together.—When safe
> from pursuit, my Father's will may be fulfilled—and I receive a
> legal claim to be the partner of your sorrows, and tenderest
> comforter.

Sheridan was too clever a man not to calculate the resonance of such
remarks, just as he was too proud a man to venture extended parallels
with his own celebrated courtship.

No character in *The Rivals* resembles Elizabeth Linley Sheridan
(though in elaborating the exchanges between Julia and Faulkland
Sheridan apparently drew on his correspondence with her in the
months before their marriage).[26] Yet Elizabeth had earlier served as
model for the central character in *The Maid of Bath*, and an understanding of the expectations Sheridan's first audiences would have taken to
performances of *The Rivals* requires some knowledge of Foote's short
play. The play suggests as well why Sheridan would have been
extremely sensitive to the indignity implicit in allowing his wife
to sing in public. First performed at the Little Theatre in the Haymarket
in June 1771, *The Maid of Bath* follows Foote's customary pattern of
broad comedy turning on a dramatization, in transparent disguise, of
persons and episodes currently the subject of public notice. Foote
depicts Elizabeth Linley—Kitty Linnet—admiringly enough, and he
takes as his satirical target Walter Long—Solomon Flint. 'I got
acquainted with Maister Foote, the play-actor,' says Lady Catherine
Coldstream (III): 'I wull [sic] get him to bring the filthy loon on the
stage—'. Flint emerges as a foolish and avaricious old man who would
purchase a beautiful girl for his wife, a project which Miss Linnet's
mother only too willingly approves; Flint appears furthermore as an
unprincipled lecher who would seduce Miss Linnet before marriage.
Foote is curiously benign in depicting the army officer who is her suitor,
Major Rackett, if he intended him, as many have assumed, to represent
Thomas Mathews. Rackett appears as a convivial and amiable, if
promiscuous, gentleman. Although Miss Linnet herself upbraids
Rackett for his earlier seduction of a milliner's apprentice, neither she
nor anyone else refers to him as a married man. On the contrary,
Sir Christopher Cripple, an elderly and wealthy man of compassion,

proposes to ease Miss Linnet's difficulties by offering Rackett two thousand pounds to marry her. She refuses because of Rackett's faults of character, and she resolutely and with dignity affirms her intention to remain unmarried and support herself by singing.

John Genest seems to have had some personal knowledge of the events depicted in the play. The idiosyncracies of his prose notwithstanding, Genest has a reputation for accuracy; and in the 1830s he resided in Bath, where his *Account of the English Stage* was published in 1832. He is certainly right in at least one telling detail: the fact that Elizabeth's mother died in 1820;[27] and he may be right in several other factual details that seem not to have been noted by Sheridan's biographers. After summarizing Foote's plot, Genest writes that

> this is very good C.[omedy]—it is founded on fact—not only the principal characters, but also the subordinate ones, were meant for persons really living at Bath—Miss Linnet was Miss Linley—the real Major Racket was a most agreeable companion, but a man of libertine principles—as he was at this time married, Foote did him too much honour when he made the Major in his drama agree to marry Miss Linnet—in July 1772 Major Racket and R. B. Sheridan fought a duel about Miss Linley—in 1773 Sheridan married her—Mrs. Linnet and Major Racket lived till 1820—Flint died in 1807; he was latterly as famous for his stinginess, as he had been in his youth for his amours.[28]

Genest would scarcely have been so precise about the dates of Long's and Mathews's deaths had he not known that he was right; and we may reasonably assume that he was accurate also in describing the personal qualities of the two men to the limited extent that oft-repeated talk about them was accurate. His report of Long emphasizes the two faults which Foote in the play also emphasizes: Long's lasciviousness and his miserliness. We can only wonder that Mr. and Mrs. Linley should have been willing, Long's wealth notwithstanding, to sacrifice their talented daughter to him.

The Maid of Bath was less than two years in the past when Sheridan married Elizabeth and less than four when he wrote *The Rivals*. The couple quickly made their way in fashionable London society, knowing that Elizabeth's misfortunes had recently been the subject of a farcical comedy, a successful one that Foote revived every summer season through 1776.[29] Although Foote depicted Elizabeth admiringly, he emphasized her poverty and her inferior social position. 'And as to yourself', 'Flint' says to 'Miss Linnet' as he attempts to seduce her (III), '(I don't speak in a disparaging way) your friends are low folks, and your fortune just nothing at all,' a statement Miss Linnet accepts as fact. One can only wonder at the genius of Elizabeth and Sheridan, who in the face of all this, in annual performances of the play, could reach the highest levels of English society.

The Rivals is different from and altogether superior to *The Maid of Bath*. But Sheridan's play is a product of experiences that followed hard on those Foote had depicted, and if Sheridan avoids Foote's kind of caricature of recognizable persons, he creates situations that in the early performances must have gained force from the inevitable associations his audiences would have made with his own and Elizabeth's recent experiences. Sheridan's method of characterization by exaggeration reaching to burlesque resembles Foote's except in the greater skill he brought to it.

Sheridan wrote *The Rivals* in haste, he explained to his father-in-law, 17 November 1774, and with the encouragement of Thomas Harris one of the proprietors of Covent Garden:

> There will be a *Comedy* of mine in rehearsal at Covent-Garden within a few days. I did not set to work on it till within a few days of my setting out for *Crome*, so you may think I have not, for these last six weeks, been very idle. I have done it at Mr. Harris's (the manager's) own request; it is now complete in his hands, and preparing for the stage. He, and some of his friends also who have heard it, assure me in the most flattering terms that there is not a doubt of its success.[30]

There was indeed to be 'a doubt of its success', its ultimate triumph notwithstanding. The doubt was owing in part to the haste with which the play was written and rehearsed. The newspaper reviewers of the first performance are all but unanimous in their criticism of the actors, especially Edward Shuter in the role of Sir Anthony, for not knowing their lines, and several of the reviewers mention as well the excessive length of the play. Sheridan's haste helps to account for the conversational fluency of the dialogue, so different from the epigrammatic style of *The School for Scandal*, and for frequency with which stock situations recur. It is difficult to think of any other Georgian play more derivative in its components than *The Rivals* and yet so original in its impact. From the expository conversation between servants in the opening scene to the antagonisms between generations, Sheridan follows familiar patterns. Yet the old seems new when Sir Anthony Absolute is the domineering father and Mrs. Malaprop her niece's equally domineering guardian. When Mrs. Malaprop reminds her niece that 'thought does not become a young woman,' we can see that Sheridan has passed beyond the conventional to an effect that is all his own.

Only eleven days separate the first and unsuccessful performance of *The Rivals* from its second and successful performance. In that brief interval, decisive for his career, Sheridan worked with the intensity he later displayed in preparing for and delivering his speeches in the indictment and in the trial of Warren Hastings. Although he regarded —and apparently with good reason[31]— some of the hostility the play had met in its first performance as having 'arisen from virulence of Malice, rather than severity of Criticism', he nevertheless heeded the criticism, he explains in his preface, and revised the play accordingly. How he revised it, he does not explain apart from alluding to two faults in the original production: the excessive length of the play and the maladroit characterization of Sir Lucius O'Trigger. In any event, much of the opposition the play had met on 17 January 1775 derived from the poor performance of the actors rather than from the play itself. By 28 January a miscasting of the role of Sir Lucius had been corrected by the substitution of Lawrence Clinch for John Lee, and all the actors knew their parts.

Our knowledge of 'the development of the text' has been enlarged by R. L. Purdy, who in 1935 published an edition of *The Rivals* which presents in parallel columns, the text as it was submitted in manuscript to the Stage Licenser and the text as it appears in the first edition, which was published on 11 February just two weeks after the successful performance of the revised play. The manuscript submitted to the Licenser presumably represents the text as the play was performed on 17 January. On the other hand, as Mr. Purdy has demonstrated, the first edition can scarcely represent the revised text performed on 28 January. The first edition seems rather to be based on an earlier manuscript than that submitted to the Licenser, a manuscript which includes passages that had been excised before the play reached the stage, as well as some of the changes Sheridan made in the latter part of January. Only the other text includes variant readings that may be attributed to Sheridan, the 'Third Edition Corrected', published early in 1777 though with the date of 1776. Although none of these texts can be regarded as a faithful representation of the play as it was performed on 28 January, Mr. Purdy has, by a comparison of them, reached convincing conclusions about some of the changes Sheridan made during those eleven days in late January 1775.[32]

The most extensive and significant changes, as we would expect, resulted from his reinterpretation of Sir Lucius O'Trigger. The character remains a proud and impecunious Irishman, quick of temper, but he has become intelligent and dignified. No longer an obtuse fortune-hunter, he is rather an Irish patriot with a keen sense of honour. More surprising are the changes made in Sir Anthony. The changes are consistent, however, with Sheridan's general practice in the revision of eliminating coarse or sexually suggestive passages. The Sir Anthony of 11 January spoke with frankness as well as vehemence; the Sir Anthony of 28 January retained his vehemence but avoided gross expressions. No doubt one of Sheridan's motives in making the changes was to avoid criticism for impropriety, but he probably wished as well to provide in Sir Anthony's polished phrases a more striking contrast to Mrs. Malaprop's elegant imprecision of diction. In any event, he excised a few malapropisms originally assigned to minor characters, presumably to accentuate those of the lady herself; and he took some of her own less sucessful ones away. He made few deletions that affected Julia and Faulkland, increasing rather than reducing the total number of their lines—an indication that the first audience found their roles more attractive than have later critics.

In view of the rapidity with which he wrote and revised *The Rivals*, it is remarkably 'regular', as a critic of the late seventeenth century might have put it. The play is unremittingly comical, coming no nearer to the subject matter of tragedy than Sir Lucius's recommendation to Bob Acres of a place for burial should he be killed in the duel: 'I'm told there is very snug lying in the Abbey.' It is comical and yet satirical, having well-defined butts of ridicule: duelling, intellectual pretentiousness, romantic indifference to financial reality, neurotic fear, and parental tyranny. Tidily though not tightly constructed, the play includes episodes and characters that could be eliminated without destroying coherence and intelligibility.[33] We would be reluctant to give up Sir Lucius, and yet his activities are but loosely joined to the principal intrigues. Even the Julia and Faulkland courtship could be cut away without destroying continuity. There is no reason to assume that Sheridan gave much attention to the dramatic 'unities'—though in the first edition a reminder appears, after the *dramatis personae*, that the unities of place and time are in fact observed. The unity of action is more problematical. In employing a primary and a secondary love intrigue Sheridan follows a pattern with a venerable history in English comedy, with the difference that he departs from the usual custom of pairing the gallants and ladies of similar disposition. He pairs them with their opposites. Although the two intrigues frequently impinge on one another, the more important link between them is in theme rather than plot, romantic fantasy in each instance blocking a desired marriage. Lydia relishes her dreams of romance; Faulkland suffers from his obsessive fears: complementary results of 'the dangerous prevalence of the imagination'.

Sheridan revised *The Rivals* in the latter part of January 1775. By May he had completed a short farce, *St. Patrick's Day*, written for the benefit night of Lawrence Clinch, the actor who in the role of Sir Lucius O'Trigger had helped save *The Rivals*. By November of the same year he had completed a comic opera, *The Duenna*, which achieved a run longer even than that of *The Beggar's Opera*. Sheridan had enormous energy as well as genius.

The letters of Sheridan, of his wife, and of his father-in-law, Thomas Linley, reveal the haste in which *The Duenna* was prepared for the stage. On 28 September, less than two months before its premiere, Linley wrote Garrick that

> . . . I have promised to assist Sheridan in compiling—I believe is the properest term—an opera; which, I understand from him, he has engaged to produce at Covent-Garden this winter. I have already set some airs which he has given me, and he intends writing new words to some other tunes of mine. My son has likewise written some tunes for him, and I understand he is to have others from Mr. Jackson of Exeter.

Linley continues, expressing to Garrick his disapproval of Sheridan's mode of procedure: 'I think he ought first to have finished his opera

with the songs he intends to introduce in it, and have got it entirely
new set'. Nevertheless, Linley explained, 'nature will not permit me
to be indifferent to his success. . . .'[34] Reluctantly, and upon the
entreaties of his daughter as well as of Sheridan, Linley gave his assistance and enlisted the assistance of his son Thomas,[35] and the preparation of the opera went on to a triumphant climax in performances
at Covent Garden beginning 21 November.

Sheridan's letters to Linley written in October and early November
provide precise instructions about the kind of tunes he wanted for his
lyrics. The first, he wrote to Linley, referring to a lyric he enclosed,
would be sung as a dialogue. 'I would wish [the tune] to be a pert,
sprightly air; for, though some of the words mayn't seem suited to it,
I should mention that they are neither of them in earnest in what they
say.'[36] (The song became the duet by Isaac and Louisa, late in Act I,
which gains force from the ironic distance between what the characters
say and what they mean.) Sheridan's letters to Linley about the music
express a depth of concern for minute detail as well as a surprising
ability to articulate the effects he desired. We may reasonably assume
that his ability to express himself on the subject, as well as his awareness
of the range of effects available to him, owed much to conversations
with his wife. If the biographical record does not allow us to know how
large a share Elizabeth Sheridan had in the composition of The Duenna,
probability would suggest that it was considerable.

An account of the music was included in a review of the opera in
The Morning Chronicle, 22 November 1775, the day after the first performance. Less approbative than we, knowing the opera's subsequent
history would expect, the author (who was probably William Wood-
fall[37]) attempted an analytical account of what he had heard:

> The music was partly composed and partly compiled: The
> Overture afforded a sample of solemn, and a sample of airy
> movements; the selected airs gave universal satisfaction though
> it was thought some of them were rather ill-adapted to the
> words they accompanied. Those that were composed did not
> please so much, and not for want of innate merit, but on account
> of their being more serious than the subject seemed to require.
> Many of the songs were admirably written; indeed some of them
> were beautifully poetical. . . .

This critic was writing about the first performance; the following day he wrote, again in *The Morning Chronicle*, about the second performance, and this time, although he did not refer specifically to the music, he was unrestrained in his praise. He commends Sheridan for having made revisions in response to the criticism the first performance had elicited. Sheridan, it would appear, had listened to and read what his critics had to say; and he had responded, as before with *The Rivals*, by making changes—though this time less extensive ones.

Sheridan's songs, too often overlooked, reveal versatility in theme and tone as well as dramatic appropriatenesses in interpretations of emotional nuances. Writing many years after Sheridan's death, William Smyth (who at Cambridge had been a tutor of one of Sheridan's sons) recorded the delight he had experienced in his youth from *The Duenna*: 'With what enjoyment . . . did I listen at the theatre of Liverpool, to Quick in the character of little Isaac, the tones of his voice, that were so irresistibly comic, conveying in the most perfect manner all the wit and humour of his sarcasms on the antiquated Duenna.'[38] The grotesquerie of Isaac's lines, conveyed not in the words themselves but in the incongruity between his lyrical tone and his age, appearance, and motive, appears among the heart-felt love songs of the young lovers. Sheridan moved easily from comic irony in some of the songs to a passionate but nearly always witty expression of emotion. And he could turn a drinking song of good fellowship as adroitly as a love song. Its satirical burden notwithstanding, the friars' song (III.v) is not unworthy of mention with the famous drinking song in *The School for Scandal* (III.iii), 'Here's to the maiden of Bashful fifteen', sung by Charles Surface's bibulous friend, Sir Toby.

'Compiling', the word Thomas Linley upon consideration selected to describe Sheridan's method of preparing *The Duenna*, had primary reference to the selection of tunes for the songs. The verb had some currency in this sense. It is so used, for example, on the title page of Isaac Bickerstaffe's *Love in the City* (1767): 'The Words Written, and the Music compiled by the Author of Love in a Village'; and it is also used in *The Morning Chronicle*, 22 November 1775, in a passage about *The Duenna* I have already quoted: 'The music was partly composed and partly compiled'. Yet if Linley was thinking primarily about Sheridan's method of assembling the music for his opera, he chose a verb that is peculiarly appropriate to Sheridan's method of contriving his plot of Spanish intrigue—if we may infer this method of composition from the completed play. The plot, though not the moral principles that control the characters' actions, is a composite of situations and episodes that in variant form had appeared in many earlier plays.

Whatever its origin, the plot—or the 'fable'—has amplitude, and it is neatly contrived. 'The fable of The Duenna', wrote the critic for *The Morning Chronicle*, 22 November 1775,

> is infinitely more substantial than that of any other musical performance we remember.—It is, in fact, so full of business and plot, that the piece might very aptly, after the manner of the managers of this Theatre, be stiled a Comedy *interspersed* with an Opera.

This is just criticism: the 'fable' of *The Duenna* is at once orderly and complex, very different from the simple plot lines of many mid-century musical plays—such as Charles Dibdin's *The Wedding Ring* (1773), from which Sheridan may have gleaned suggestions. The ingenuity of design revealed in *The Duenna*, in which 'Spanish' intrigue is not inconsistent with intelligibility, provides a principal source of our pleasure in it. The plot, though not the mocking tone which Sheridan sometimes employs, is typical of the Spanish cape and sword plays, and the English adaptations and imitations of them, written during the preceding century.[39]

The reviewer of *The Duenna* in *The Morning Chronicle*, 22 November 1775, in fact remarked that 'The story of it greatly resembles the story of a Spanish Play to be met with in a collection of French translations of Theatrical Pieces, entitled *Le Théatre Espagnol*...'. A collection of plays with precisely that title had been published in Paris in 1770; and although *The Duenna* resembles several plays in it in a generalized way, I would be reluctant to say that its plot 'greatly resembles the story' of any one of them. Many Spanish plays—Calderón's *La dama duende*, *Mañanas de abril y mayo*, and *El escondido y la tapada*, for example— turn on just such deceptions and disguises as those in *The Duenna*. (*El escondido y la tapada*, in an adaptation by Isaac Bickerstaffe entitled *'Tis Well It's No Worse*, had been produced at Drury Lane as recently as November 1770.[40]) Moreto's *El lindo don Diego* includes the motif of a gentleman courting a servant woman, believing her to be a lady. It is not impossible that Sheridan used a single 'source' play, but I think it

unlikely. In reading and rereading *The Duenna*, I have been consistently reminded of earlier plays, English, Spanish, and French; in trying
to find a 'source' for it, following leads from remarks of eighteenth-
century critics and modern works of reference, I have been as consistently
frustrated. No single earlier play, to my knowledge, uses the conventional complications of plot, character relationships, and episodes
in a pattern anticipating Sheridan's.

The Duenna opens with a nocturnal scene similar to the opening
scene of many Spanish plays; and most though not all the characters
correspond to character types of the *comedia*. Lopez, a servant who
resembles the Spanish type of the *gracioso*, complains as he waits for his
master outside of a darkened house in Seville, that his master, Ferdinand,
'is much too gallant to eat, drink or sleep'—a sentiment frequently
expressed by similar characters in Spanish drama, who share some of the
attitudes of Cervantes's Sancho Panza. Antonio, a young gentleman,
comes to serenade his beloved, Louisa, who is the sister of Ferdinand.
Conventions of the Spanish cape and sword plays recur throughout
the opera: serenades in the night, disguises and mistakes in identity,
intrigues by young lovers to thwart the matrimonial plans made for
them by their elders.

The resemblances of *The Duenna* to earlier plays made Sheridan
vulnerable, even more perhaps than in *The Rivals*, *The School for
Scandal*, and *The Critic*, to charges of plagiarism. Yet so far as has been
determined, his literary debt is no greater than that of most other
eighteenth-century dramatists who wrote in a well-defined tradition
—here that of the Spanish intrigue play.

Paradoxically it is an English adaptation from the Italian rather than
from the Spanish that most significantly anticipates the plot and the
operatic form of *The Duenna*: Charles Dibdin's short 'Comic Opera'
The Wedding Ring of 1773, which derives from Goldoni's *Il filosofo di
campagna*. A much slighter piece than *The Duenna*, *The Wedding Ring*,
with only five characters, moves on a simple plot in which a young
gentlewoman, Felicia, and her maidservant, Lissetta, frustrate the
plans of Felicia's father, Pandolfo, to marry her to the rich Zerbino in
order that she can marry the man of her choice, Henrico. Lissetta,
pretending to be her mistress, receives Zerbino (whom she had des-
scribed as possessing 'more money than understanding') as her suitor.
When Zerbino kisses her, she warns him about her pretended father,
Pandolfo: 'Why he intends to trap you into marriage with my maid.'

When in consequence of this warning Zerbino refuses to accept Felicia, her father allows her to marry Henrico. Zerbino, entrapped into marriage with Lissetta, accepts her in good grace when he is undeceived. The fact that *The Wedding Ring* is a successful comic opera that was performed many times between its opening in February 1773 and October 1774, less than a year before Sheridan was at work on his own comic opera, lends plausibility to a guess that he took suggestions from it.

He may have taken suggestions as well from Sir William Davenant's *The Man's the Master*, 1668, which was revived at Covent Garden on 3 November 1775, eighteen days before the première of *The Duenna* at the same theatre. Although the men rather than the women reverse roles in *The Man's the Master*, and in this respect *The Duenna* resembles the play less obviously than it does *The Wedding Ring*, Davenant exploits far more extensively than Dibdin the comic potential inherent in a courtship like that in *The Duenna* in which one of the individuals is deceived about the identity and the social rank of the other. Sheridan could scarcely have avoided seeing *The Man's the Master* either in rehearsal or in performance while he himself was at Covent Garden 'compiling', as his father-in-law put it, *The Duenna*; and in elaborating the splendidly ridiculous scenes of Isaac Mendoza's courtship of the aging and homely Margaret, his title character, he may well have had in mind the comic absurdities that arise when Davenant's loutish servant, Jodelet, pays court to the beautiful Isabella. The farcical scenes notwithstanding, *The Man's the Master* is in the specialized seventeenth- and eighteenth-century sense of the term a 'Spanish plot'; in this instance one that is little more than a free translation of a play by Paul Scarron, which in turn is an adaptation of one by Francisco de Rojas Zorrilla.[41] *The Man's the Master*, to cite but one example of a recurrent situation in the Spanish intrigue plays, opens as *The Duenna* opens with a nocturnal scene outside a lady's house. A servant voices the simple needs of bodily comfort while awaiting his master, in whom romantic love has displaced other human needs.

Charles Dibdin, as the author or translator of *The Wedding Ring* and the composer of the songs in it, had as good a claim as anyone to regard himself as a dramatist who had supplied Sheridan with suggestions for *The Duenna*. Whether from resentment of Sheridan's unacknowledged debt, if indeed there was one, or some other unknown reason, Dibdin in his autobiographical series of 'letters', *The Musical Tour* (1788),

reveals a sustained hostility to Sheridan which takes the form of stated
or implied accusations of plagiarism in a vein not unlike that of Gerard
Langbaine in the seventeenth century writing about John Dryden.[42]
Curiously, however, in his extended account of the 'sources' of *The
Duenna*, although he refers to Goldoni's *Il filosofo di campagna*, he makes
no reference to his own comic opera based on it.[43] (Elsewhere in his
volume he refers to Goldoni's play as the source for *The Wedding Ring*
but without mentioning *The Duenna*.[44]) His list of the literary antecedents of *The Duenna* has a limited usefulness similar to that of Langbaine's comments on Dryden's plays. As a contemporary's guide
to works now little known, Dibdin can point our way to profitable
investigation provided we keep in mind that hostility led him to dog-
matic overstatement.

It is not profitable to consider all the works Dibdin mentions; but
one of them invites comment, Susanna Centlivre's *The Wonder: A
Woman Keeps a Secret* (1714), which in its continuing popularity on the
eighteenth-century stage was a force in perpetuating the 'Spanish plot'.
In the second half of the century, when Garrick and later John Philip
Kemble often took the principal role, it was performed almost two
hundred times.[45] Probably Sheridan had some knowledge of *The
Wonder* as early as 1775. In any event, there are extended parallels
between Mrs. Centlivre's two plot lines and two of the three in *The
Duenna*.

Don Felix and Isabella in *The Wonder*, like Ferdinand and Louisa in
The Duenna, are brother and sister, children of a stern father who is
determined to marry his beautiful daughter against her will to a rich
man. In each instance the man is so repugnant to the daughter that she
flees her father's house to escape marriage. The father of Violante, the
second young woman in *The Wonder*, like the father (and stepmother)
of Clara in *The Duenna*, attempts to force her to become a nun. In the
two works, Felix and Ferdinand love Violante and Clara respectively;
an English colonel and Antonio love Isabella and Louisa respectively
The stratagems employed by Mrs. Centlivre's and by Sheridan's young
couples to escape parental tyranny and achieve their desired marriages
differ in detail but are alike in comforming to conventions of intrigue
recurrent in the Spanish plays.

Yet the impression produced by the early eighteenth-century play
and the late eighteenth-century opera on a reader (and, we may assume,
on an audience) are unlike—so unlike as to provide insight into the

nature of Sheridan's reinterpretation of the 'Spanish plot'. Sheridan's use of the Spanish conventions is not unlike his use of the conventions of comedy of manners in *The Rivals*: he exaggerates them to the edge of burlesque. The confusions and mistakes in identity come so fast in *The Duenna* as to approach the farcical. If the relationships among the major characters approximate those of the Spanish cape and sword plays and the English imitations of them such as Mrs. Centlivre's *The Wonder*, Sheridan departs radically from the Spanish ethos. His is a world of intrigue bordering on farce that is closer in tone to the improvised intrigue of the Italian *commedia dell' arte* than to the courtly and decorous intrigue of the Spanish cape and sword play, in which comic situations, however prominent, are not inconsistent with reverence for family honour.

I cannot say with certainty that Sheridan took suggestions for *The Duenna* from either Dibdin's *The Wedding Ring* or from Mrs. Centlivre's *The Wonder*. Probably he drew from both of them, but proof is lacking. Yet it is instructive to note that Sheridan, like Dibdin in his comic opera based on an Italian play having some resemblances to *commedia dell'arte*, portrays characters who are little troubled by social rank and personal distinction in the choice of marriage partners for their children or themselves. Don Jerome, the father of Louisa in *The Duenna*, chooses for his daughter Isaac Mendoza, a Jew of grotesque appearance who has recently and conveniently been converted to Christianity, because he is rich. When Zerbino, the rich but dim-witted heir in *The Wedding Ring*, is entrapped into marriage with the servingmaid Lissetta (a misalliance of a kind that is all but non-existent in Restoration and eighteenth-century comedy of native English origin), he accepts her without apparent concern for his family honour. On the other hand, the avaricious father Don Lopez of *The Wonder*, although as insensitive to his daughter Isabella's wishes as Sheridan's Don Jerome, chooses as his son-in-law a man who is high born as well as rich. When an English merchant, Frederick, an honourable man of strong good sense, expostulates to Don Lopez (I.i) that he would sacrifice his beautiful daughter 'to Age, Avarice, and a Fool', the father acknowledges 'the justness of the Character', but counters that the man is rich and of suitable rank, qualities 'which render him very agreeable to me for a Son-in-Law'. Mrs. Centlivre takes over, not merely the conventions of intrigue and character relationships of the Spanish *comedia*, but in modified form at least its animating spirit: an

F

unyielding and sometimes an irrational devotion to family honour and reputation.

In the Spanish plays a prudent concern for property settlements need not be incompatible with regard for family honour. But money does not determine all decisions as it does among the older generation in *The Duenna*. The father and stepmother of Clara try to force her into a convent so that the family property can be inherited by the child of the father's second marraige; Louisa's father has chosen Isaac Mendoza, for financial reasons alone, to become her husband; Isaac in his turn is willing to marry the duenna, her age and appearance notwithstanding, because he mistakenly believes her to be the heiress Louisa whom he can marry secretly without making a property settlement on her. To Sheridan the 'Spanish plot' was merely a convenient vehicle to carry his splendid succession of comically absurd situations and poignant lyrical interludes, the absurd and the lyrical in their turn being intensified by the songs.

Whatever we may conclude about Sheridan's literary sources for *The Duenna*, there can be no doubt that the pattern of Spanish intrigue he employed—though not the comic or satirical use he made of it—is a reworking of dramatic formulae popular on the English stage since the 1660s. Even so, the opera, like *The Rivals* of a few months earlier, includes situations that put us in mind of Sheridan's and Elizabeth's experiences before they were married. Don Jerome's decision that Louisa should marry Isaac Mendoza seems little more bizarre than had been Thomas Linley's decision that Elizabeth should marry Walter Long.

Like Elizabeth before her, Louisa flees from her father's house to escape the attentions of a suitor (Thomas Mathews—Isaac Mendoza) and takes refuge in a convent. Safely there, both girls—the one who became Sheridan's wife and her dramatic counterpart—write reassuring letters to their fathers.[46] Louisa has a mature understanding of the importance of money for happiness in marriage that, though different from the avarice of her elders in the play, would seem to be not unlike that possessed by the sensible even if romantically-disposed Elizabeth. 'I do not doubt your sincerity, Antonio:' Louisa says (III.iii), 'but there is a chilling air around poverty that often kills affection, that was not nurs'd in it—'.

To soften the force of her reminder that even lovers must have a means of subsistence, Louisa sings to Antonio—as we can imagine that Elizabeth had sung to Sheridan—proclaiming the wealth inherent in their love. Commenting on the love songs in *The Duenna*, Thomas Moore (himself certainly an authority on the love song), wrote that 'It is impossible to believe' that some of them

> had no deeper inspiration than the imaginary loves of an opera. They bear, burnt into every line, the marks of personal feeling, and must have been thrown off in one of those passionate moods of the heart, with which the poet's own youthful love had made him acquainted. . . .[47]

We are easily convinced that Moore was right, even without such corroborative evidence as surviving manuscripts provide.[48]

Just as in Faulkland of *The Rivals*, we may suspect, though without firm assurance, that there is an autobiographical strain in Ferdinand, the self-tormenting lover of Clara. In his brooding anxieties, Ferdinand bears a curious resemblance to the earlier character, and like him may owe his being—more strictly his temperament—to the melancholic strain in Sheridan himself. In any event, Ferdinand and Antonio provide a contrast in personality resembling that between Faulkland and Jack Absolute. In his love for Clara, Ferdinand is jealous even of Antonio, who loves Ferdinand's sister, Louisa. Antonio has the robust common sense of Jack Absolute. Antonio refused to suffer for a lady, he explains first in dialogue and then in a song (I.ii), who would not return his affection:

> I ne'er could any lustre see
> In eyes that wou'd not look on me. . . .

Yet it is Isaac Mendoza, not Antonio, who provides a comic counterbalance to the lyrical idealism of the lovers. Isaac's grotesque courtship of the title character, Margaret, functions as contrast to the affectionate courtship of the two young couples: a mercenary and deceitful courtship of superannuated 'lovers' contrasted with the spontaneous courtship of the young. The portrait of Isaac, no more subtle than those of Sir Anthony Absolute and Mrs. Malaprop in *The Rivals*, is like them a caricature. Sheridan succeeds with Isaac, as he had succeeded with the elderly pair in *The Rivals*, by his resourceful audacity in exaggerating a trait of personality: here an avarice that conquers all. Isaac carries on a dialogue with himself, expressing his true thoughts (usually in asides, occasionally in conversation), allowing us to observe the conflict within his mind between his spontaneous emotions and his pervasive avarice; but we are never in doubt that greed will prevail. And we can be sure that in performance clever singers captured the ambiguity of his responses. Sheridan, like all masters in the art of burlesque, succeeds by his choice of those details which will convey a single impression.

That *The Duenna* was superbly entertaining in performance we cannot doubt. The surviving testimony of those who saw and heard it and the objective record of its popularity[49] are convincing. Yet students of the drama, when they think of it at all, think of it as a phenomenon of dramatic history rather than as a living presence in the theatre. Its reputation in our time is totally different from that of *The Beggar's Opera*, the only musical comedy which in popularity rivalled *The Duenna* in the eighteenth century. Even apart from its separate life in Berthold Brecht's adaptation as *Die Dreigroschenoper*, *The Beggar's Opera* continues to be performed by professional and amateur companies alike, it has appeared as a motion picture, and it is included in nearly every comprehensive anthology of eighteenth-century plays. We may reasonably ask why the difference in the fate of the two operas.

The difference arises, I think, from the striking contrast between them in their intellectual, more precisely their satirical, dimensions. Of all Sheridan's dramatic works, *The Duenna* is most innocent of thought on serious subjects. Occasional pungent observations appear in dialogue, as in Don Jerome's remark (II.iii) that 'nobility, without an estate is as ridiculous as gold-lace on a frize-coat', but these are asides in conversational exchanges on other subjects. Sheridan's hostile depiction of the Roman Catholic clergy, in a scene (III.v) which has no functional relationship to the plot, seems to be a gratuitous exploitation of English prejudice to raise an easy laugh.[50] So too the anti-Semitism inherent in the characterization of Isaac Mendoza. The mocking portrait of the newly-converted Jew would seem to represent no more than the thoughtless acceptance of a literary convention.

The absence of a satirical dimension in *The Duenna* becomes the more apparent when we think of the satirical audacity of *The Beggar's Opera*. Gay wrote before the Licensing Act and after the custom of licensing by the Master of the Revels had fallen into disuse.[51] He enjoyed a freedom to comment on English institutions and even on individuals (including the King's first minister, Sir Robert Walpole) denied to dramatists writing later in the century. In his satirical stratagem of inverting social rank, Gay comes strangely close to the line, without passing over it, that separates laughing criticism of the structure of society from militant advocacy of revolutionary change.[52] Gay's probing of political, social, and personal relationships has a permanent relevance to men's affairs transcending his comment on the politics of Walpole's England.

The Duenna has a more substantial and a more neatly contrived plot than The Beggar's Opera. Yet in comparison with the earlier play, it seems curiously remote from serious human concerns of the eighteenth or of the twentieth century. To be sure, it sustains a satirical comment on the power of wealth to corrupt human relationships— above all, the most intimate relationship, marriage. But this is a familiar subject, not here redeemed by originality of treatment. Even during the opera's early popularity, the deficiency in provocative ideas elicited comment. In a review of The School for Scandal, The Morning Chronicle, 9 May 1777, a critic concluded his remarks on that play with a qualified prophecy that it would become 'as great a favourite as the Duenna to which it is infinitely superior in point of sense, satire, and moral.'[53] This is the understatement of a cautious man. We can admire the craftsmanship that shaped the plot of The Duenna, which is always busy, always intelligible, and frequently comical, and yet regard the opera as a museum piece, in which serious comment on human affairs has little part.

In his other dramatic works, Sheridan more nearly escapes from the blandness that is the consequence of an insufficiency of ideas. He is never an insistent moralist or an audacious investigator of social relationships, but elsewhere he writes more cogently about important subjects: in The Rivals the perennial tensions between the generations and the role of fantasy in courtship; in The School for Scandal the malice that finds expression in hypocritical gossip; in The Critic the professional and literary problems that complicated the life of the proprietor of a theatre. We must take The Duenna as it is, an amusing libretto to read and one that in performance delighted two generations of Englishmen.

4

The Survival of Neoclassicism, *A Trip to Scarborough* and *The School for Scandal*

The perennial comparisons of *The School for Scandal* to Restoration comedy are not fanciful despite Sheridan's firm base in Georgian comic tradition. Nor is the conventional grouping of plays 'from Dryden to Sheridan' in university courses of study without a logic of its own, independent of academic convenience. Major changes in comedy occurred during the century, of course; but Sheridan represents the end of an era in dramatic history as clearly as Dryden represents its beginning.

What are we to call this era? The absence of an inclusive and generally acceptable term such as 'Renaissance' (which is used without major dissent to describe as long a span of dramatic history as that separating Dryden and Sheridan) is more than a casual inconvenience. There is no agreement on how far chronologically we may extend the term 'Restoration,' which is not strictly accurate if applied to the work of Congreve, whose first play appeared five years after the Revolution. No one would venture to describe *The School for Scandal* as a 'Restoration' comedy, but many use the word in referring to comedies written during Queen Anne's reign. Can we find a less ambiguous adjective? 'Augustan' is a possibility. Yet even apart from its dubious appropriateness when applied to such comedies as those of Vanbrugh and Farquhar, it suggests a time span—late seventeenth and early eighteenth centuries—different from but no less restricted than "Restoration." We are left with the ponderous phrase 'Restoration and Eighteenth Century,' awkward in university catalogues and even more awkward in the titles of books and essays.

Perhaps we should reconsider 'neoclassical'—so long at least as we confine attention to the drama. The term has become controversial, and I must use it with caution. James William Johnson has reminded us of the complexity of the origins of the literature we customarily call neoclassical.[1] Donald Greene has argued that the term is inapplicable and even misleading as a general description of literature as diverse as that produced in England between 1660 and 1800.[2] Bertrand H. Bronson perfers the simpler term 'classical,' arguing that the prefix is redundant and inaccurate—though I think it fair to add that he uses it in the title of his essay ('When was Neoclassicism?') as a means of suggesting precisely what his subject is.[3] Robert D. Hume has reminded us, and in doing so clarified the problem, that in using the adjective 'neoclassical' we should differentiate 'between *the nature of a work of art* and the *cultural orientation* of the artist'.[4] I cannot attempt to summarize, much less to answer, the complex and subtle arguments of these scholars, many of which I find convincing. Certainly I agree that the adjective offers problems, more of them than we realized a few years ago. Yet in discussing the history of drama, a much more restricted subject than general literary or intellectual history, I am reluctant to give it up, so accurately does it describe a set of assumptions that writers from Dryden to Sheridan took as the point of departure for the innovations that give their plays individuality. The term, prefix and all, is particularly useful, I think, because it emphasizes the conscious effort to adapt to the modern situation a literary theory assumed to have been formulated by the Ancients.

The history of drama from 1660 to 1779 presents a simpler problem in terminology than that provided by non-dramatic literature, and the problem is the more intelligible because we can refer to a large body of criticism written by contemporaries. Criticism of the drama appears earlier in the Restoration than criticism of other forms of literature, and from the time of Dryden to that of Sheridan it was voluminous. It was also consistently preoccupied with the relationship between modern drama and the drama of Antiquity. Dryden employed as an organizing principle in *Of Dramatic Poesy*, as everyone knows, a comparison of modern drama—English, French, and to some extent Spanish—with Greek and Roman drama. Dryden and his younger contemporaries Thomas Rymer and John Dennis studied the French criticism written by such men as Pierre Corneille and René Rapin, who in turn made frequent reference to the drama and criticism of Antiquity. Throughout the later seventeenth century English critics were pre-occupied with conceptions of genre, plot construction, and didactic strategy which were assumed to have ancient precedent. The Jeremy Collier controversy at century's end was conducted on both sides with attention to the brief remarks on comedy in Aristotle's *Poetics* and to the voluminous commentary they had elicited. The discussion of Steele's innovations in comedy turned partly on differing attitudes toward their relationship to ancient drama. Steele cited Terence in defense of *The Conscious Lovers*; Dennis in opposition cited Aristotle. As I have already said, the differences between Steele and Dennis have a close parallel fifty years later in the differences between Cumberland and Goldsmith. Sheridan's protests against what he considered to be sentimental comedy were grounded in the classical differentiation between the dramatic genres.[5]

This is not to say that the dramatists wrote their plays with close attention to neoclassical principles. Criticism of comedy was often evoked by infringements, or alleged infringements, of neoclassical precept: in the Restoration, by the mingling of the genres in tragi-comedy and by the casualness or indifference of some writers to the didactic function of drama; in the eighteenth century, by the intro-duction of scenes of emotional intensity and by the preference often shown for the exemplary over the satirical method of conveying moral instruction. Nevertheless, with remarkable consistency the innovations in comedy were examined by contemporaries with reference to ancient drama and dramatic theory.

On the evidence of *The Critic* alone, we could assert that Sheridan's conception of comedy was neoclassical as that conception had been given definition in seventeenth-century French and English criticism. And when we turn to his five-act comedies—*The Rivals*, *A Trip to Scarborough*, and *The School for Scandal*—we may well conclude that he took the neoclassical premises more seriously in writing his plays than had the principal comic dramatists of the Restoration.

Mr. Bronson has provided a salutary warning, in the essay to which I have referred entitled 'When Was Neoclassicism?', against believing that the history of English literature from 1660 to 1800 supports the assumption that there was a consistent movement 'from classic to romantic'. 'For a while,' he writes, 'I was tempted to take as my title,

"From Romantic to Classic," thinking thereby to point the moral in a ready and easy way.'[6] Mr. Bronson does not refer to the history of comedy, but we may find in it support for his thesis.

I can illustrate the survival, even the intensification, of the hold of neoclassical ideals by referring comparatively to the first great dramatist to emerge after 1660, Dryden, and the last to write before 1800, Sheridan. Dryden wrote or wrote part of a dozen comedies: two adaptations of famous comic plots of the past, *The Tempest* and *Amphitryon*, three satirical or farcical comedies of London life, *The Wild Gallant, Sir Martin Mar-all*, and *The Kind Keeper*, and seven tragicomedies, *The Rival Ladies, Secret Love, An Evening's Love, Marriage A-la-Mode, The Assignation, The Spanish Friar*, and *Love Triumphant*. With the single exception of *Amphitryon*, the better of these plays are all tragicomedies—that is to say, plays in which the generic distinction between tragedy and comedy is blurred. Dryden knew that in them he was vulnerable to critics of a neoclassical turn of mind, such critics as those he represented imaginatively in *Of Dramatic Poesy* in the figure of Lisideius, the spokesman for French theory and practice; and throughout his career he included in his essays statements defending tragicomedy. It is notable, however, that the tone of those statements changes with the passage of years, growing more apologetic. From Neander's exposition in *Of Dramatic Poesy* of the rationale for tragicomedy, concluding with the boast that 'to the honour of our nation, . . . we have invented, increased, and perfected a more pleasant way of writing for the stage than was ever known to the ancients or moderns of any nation, which is tragicomedy,'[7] we move some thirteen years later to the cautious and prudential statement in the dedication to *The Spanish Friar* that he had satisfied his 'humour, which was to tack two plays together; and to break a rule for the pleasure of variety'.[8] In the interval Rymer had published his translation of Rapin's *Reflections on Aristotle's Treatise of Poesie* and his own *Tragedies of the Last Age*, works that made a deep impression on Dryden as well as other Restoration dramatists.

Dryden was vulnerable and knew that he was vulnerable to objections that he had blended the genres of tragedy and comedy; he was also vulnerable, and knew that he was, to objections that he had slighted the didactic function of comedy. It was not that he disagreed in principle with the commonplace of literary criticism that comedy, like other forms of literature, should be instructive, though in the preface to

An Evening's Love he remarks that instruction could at most be 'its secondary end'.[9] All four of the interlocutors in *Of Dramatic Poesy* accept Lisideius's description of drama which concludes with a phrase about the purpose for which it is written: *'for the delight and instruction of mankind'*.[10] And long before Jeremy Collier's polemic, Dryden included in his Killigrew ode an acknowledgment of guilt, his own and his fellow dramatists', in having contributed to 'the steaming Ordures of the Stage'.[11] Unlike the other important dramatists attacked by Collier, Dryden made only a tentative defence, and in the preface to the *Fables* pleaded guilty.[12]

Now consider Sheridan. It is sufficiently obvious that he had a more restrictive notion of the genre of comedy than Dryden; the point does not require argument. So too the didactic strategy of his plays is less ambiguous. Sheridan's didactic methods are not unlike those which several of the Restoration dramatists, including Vanbrugh, professed to follow in defending themselves in the Collier controversy. There is a certain disingenuousness in some of the late seventeenth-century assertions that the dramatists had served Christian morality by depicting vice as odious. We are disinclined to admire Collier and his disciple Steele, but—within the critical and religious context in which the Collier controversy was carried on—there was force in their argument that the prosperity awarded the rake heroes at play's end was a fault. If we do not find *The Man of Mode* and *The Relapse* morally offensive, let us remember that we do not accept the premises held or allegedly held by the dramatists and the reformers alike. Ben Jonson and Molière had indeed written plays that supported Christian morality, and the same can be said, with qualifications, of Wycherley, but scarcely, without major qualifications, of Dryden, Etherege, and even Congreve. In Sheridan, on the other hand, the moral basis for judging character is as unambiguous as it is in Molière.

Sheridan's affinity with Molière merits emphasis. In his didactic strategy he resembles Molière more closely than Congreve, to whose plays his own best comedy is inevitably compared. In most though not all respects in which Sheridan departed from Restoration practice, he had a precedent, whether he knew it or not, in Molière. The nature and quality of Sheridan's neoclassicism will be more apparent if we think of his plays, not merely in relation to Restoration comedy, but also in relation to Molière. *The School for Scandal* in particular recalls Molière— specifically, *L'École des femmes*; more generally, the so-called thesis plays in which a well-defined vice is systematically ridiculed. At least one contemporary critic noted the resemblance between the two dramatists, a reviewer writing in *The Gazetteer and New Daily Advertiser*, 10 May 1777:

> . . . the perplexities of the plot [in *The School for Scandal*] are
> . . . not only contrived in the most striking, but regular manner;
> —a superior excellence scarcely known to the ancients, and
> attained by Molliere alone among the moderns.

And this critic, whose review was published just two days after the first performance of the play, added to his praise of Sheridan's 'regular manner', a further comparison of Sheridan's 'wit' to that of Congreve:

> The piece abounds with manly sentiments, intirely divested of
> affectation, and which are conveyed to the heart through the
> purest channels of wit. In this particular Congreve eclipsed the
> fame of all his predecessors, no nation excepted. . . . They who
> have a sufficient knowledge of literature, will not offer to con-
> test that Congreve sits unrivalled on the throne of dramatic wit:
> —and if any author has a right to dispute Congreve's royal
> supremacy, it is the Writer of The School for Scandal.

Sheridan, in brief, has rivalled Congreve's 'wit' even as he has equalled Molière's accomplishment in dramatic structure.

Sheridan wrote his plays with a more restrictive and specifically neoclassical conception of the genre of comedy than that of Dryden when he wrote his plays. But can we say the same if we compare Sheridan with the other principal Restoration dramatists? I think so— and so apparently did the reviewer for *The Gazetteer and New Daily Advertiser*. Vanbrugh's *The Relapse* may fairly be considered if not typical at least representative of the best in late seventeenth-century comedy, and we may gain from a comparison of that play and Sheridan's adaptation of it some understanding of the two dramatists' attitudes toward neoclassicism.

Let me say at once that I think Sheridan wrote his adaptation of *The Relapse* on principles analogous to those controlling many Restoration and eighteenth-century adaptations of Shakespeare. He refashioned the earlier play to make it conform, or more nearly conform, to the

unities of time, place, and action; he removed ambiguities of motivation and event; he removed what he apparently thought were offensive
—that is, indecorous—expressions; and he reworked the denouement
to make the plot a more obvious recommendation of Christian
morality. Furthermore, in at least one striking episode, he reduced the
emotional intensity of the original, eliminating a passage that we would
be inclined to call 'sentimental' had it not been written by Vanbrugh.

The changes he made are concisely described in a review printed in
The Morning Chronicle, 25 February 1777:

> The chief alterations, (exclusive of verbal corrections and
> several additional speeches) consist of the removal of the first
> scene of the Relapse, the change of the sex of Coupler, the giving
> Worthy the name of Col. Townly, calling the Surgeon Mr.
> Probe, abridging the 4th act, introducing an entire new scene
> in the fifth, producing the *denouement* in a different and improved
> manner, and preserving the unity of place by laying the scene
> altogether in the country.[13]

It should also be noted that Sheridan avoided the loose blank verse—
sometimes distinguishable from prose only by typographical convention—to which Vanbrugh turned in several lyrical or mock-lyrical
episodes.

We will continue to prefer *The Relapse* to *A Trip to Scarborough*, just
as we will more emphatically prefer *The Country Wife* to Garrick's *The
Country Girl*. The eighteenth-century plays are innocuous in comparison with their originals, lacking the central and disturbing satirical
insights which animate the earlier plays. In reducing Pinchwife from
husband to guardian, and even more in eliminating the role of Horner,
Garrick obscured the vision of hypocrisy that controls Wycherley's
play. In reworking the character of Loveless, Sheridan obscured the
insight that prompted Vanbrugh's critique of Cibber's *Love's Last
Shift*: the impossibility of a hardened libertine's abrupt transformation
into a devoted husband. We prefer Vanbrugh's uninhibited depiction
of sexual subjects to Sheridan's muted and at times evasive depiction of
them. *A Trip to Scarborough* is most frequently criticized as a bowdlerization of *The Relapse*. The criticism is just, but more needs to be said on
the subject. Let us remember that the comedies of Molière are restrained
in references to sexual relations. Sheridan had honourable precedent for
his restraint.

In any event, if he wished to make use of Vanbrugh's play, he was compelled by the reticences of the Georgian audience to make changes in it. 'The *Trip to Scarborough*, presented last night at Drury-Lane Theatre,' wrote a reviewer for *The Morning Chronicle*, 25 February 1777,

> is an alteration of the comedy of the RELAPSE, which was not only replete with gross allusions, but exhibited so glaring a picture of vice and immorality, that it has long been deemed unfit for representation. Mr. Sheridan . . . has, (considering the heap of indecency he had to remove,) achieved an Herculean task,

though, the reviewer added, 'we fear to very little purpose'. The play's cool reception, however, seems to have been largely the fault of the actors. On 28 March 1777, *The Gazetteer and New Daily Advertiser* reported that 'The third representation of the Trip to Scarborough last night, met with the most favourable reception from a splendid and crowded audience. The performers being more familiar with their parts than on the first and second nights, the auditors had a better opportunity of discovering all the merit of the piece.' Our modern preference for Vanbrugh notwithstanding, *A Trip to Scarborough* indeed has merit.

In at least one instance, we may consider Sheridan's bowdlerization as gain. Even in this emancipated age, many do not relish the depiction of male homosexuality. The usual avoidance of the subject in sub-literary pornographic novels, many of which are structured as a succession of episodes portraying varieties of sexual gratfication (including lesbianism) provides the evidence of the market place that the subject is repulsive. Restoration audiences seem to have found it so. For all the boldness of the comic dramatists in the portrayal of illicit sexual relations (and couples in the plays of Etherege and Wycherley do not always stop just in time), it is difficult to find in a comedy produced in the theatre between 1660 and 1696 such an overt exhibition of male homosexuality as Coupler's advances to Young Fashion in *The Relapse*. Incest in tragedy and incest averted in comedy are frequent motifs, the latter in fact a recurrent motif in the plays of Dryden, but not overt homosexuality. There are occasional hints of it in tragedy, in Dryden's *All for Love*, for example, and Lee's *The Rival Queens*, but little more than hints. Sheridan avoids the subject in *A*

Trip to Scarborough by the simple expedient of transforming Coupler into an old woman.

We regret Sheridan's modifications in the depiction of heterosexual relations—but again there is ample Restoration precedent for the last minute avoidance of fornication or adultery. Except in two of his inferior comedies which were not altogether his own work, Dryden's longing couples do not commit adultery. Dryden is not typical in this respect, though the other dramatists consistently preserve the chastity of their heroines. Vanbrugh's Amanda does not fall, though her husband succumbs to the enticing widow Berenthia in one of the funniest scenes of the play: the famous episode in which, with her protests growing ever more faint, he carries her off the stage. 'Help, help,' Berenthia cries out *'Very softly,'* 'I'm Ravish'd, ruin'd, undone! O Lord, I shall never be able to bear it.' This is lost in *A Trip to Scarborough*, and the resorting of the couples to their proper mates is accomplished in dialogue unpleasantly reminiscent of *Love's Last Shift*. The mutual agreement of the two couples to respect each other's rights is moderately convincing, at least as convincing as the similar agreement in *Marriage A-la-Mode*.

In censuring Sheridan for what seems an evasion of the sexual theme implied in the title of *The Relapse*—that is, the impossibility of an instantaneous change in personality of such an experienced rake as Loveless—we must remember that *A Trip to Scarborough*, unlike Vanbrugh's play, is not a sequel to *Love's Last Shift*. *The Relapse* was performed in the same year as Cibber's play, at a time when audiences could be presumed to recognize the Loveless of the later play as that of the earlier. Vanbrugh recalls his character's past history when Loveless tells Amanda about his experience at the theatre (II), 'I happen'd in the Play to find my very Character, only with the addition of a *Relapse* . . .', a mirror image accentuating Vanbrugh's critical objective. Sheridan's Loveless, having no record of prolonged libertinism, can appear as no more vulnerable to a pretty and receptive young woman than any other warm-blooded husband: that is to say, very vulnerable, but not depraved beyond recognition of his wife's claim on him. His return to marital fidelity can come as no more of a shock to our sense of psychological probability than that of Rhodophil in *Marriage A-la-Mode*.

Several of the more important differences between Vanbrugh's and Sheridan's plays derive from the fact that the one but not the other is a parody of an earlier play, and in plot, characterization, and dialogue is partially controlled by Vanbrugh's parodic design. Like Fielding in *Joseph Andrews*, Vanbrugh takes the earlier work as his point of departure, and after an initial passage devoted to it, turns to other concerns, reverting infrequently to parody. Scarcely less than *Joseph Andrews*, *The Relapse* offers problems of differentiating the results of rapid if brilliant improvisation from calculated design. Did Fielding when he began to write intend to subordinate Joseph's experiences with Lady Booby to the depiction of Parson Adams, who has no antecedent in Richardson's novel? Did Vanbrugh intend, in portraying the sudden repentance of Worthy, a burlesque of Cibber's portrayal of Loveless' conversion? Whatever Vanbrugh's intentions, his play includes ambiguities that Sheridan took care to remove.

In his reestablishment of domestic harmony at play's end, Sheridan passes over the final confrontation between Amanda and Worthy, whom he has renamed Colonel Townly. When in a passionate scene Vanbrugh's Worthy is repulsed and abandoned by Amanda even though she knows her husband has passed beyond redemption, Worthy praises her in a soliloquy that we would call 'sentimental' if it had been written by Cibber (V.iv):

> Sure there's Divinity about her; and sh'as dispenc'd some portion on't to me. For what but now was the wild flame of Love, or (to dissect that specious term) The Vile, the gross desires of Flesh and Blood, is in a moment turn'd to Adoration.[14]

Is this burst of emotional extravagance to be interpreted as burlesque of Cibber's denouement? Yet apart from the luxuriance of the imagery, there is no signal from the dramatist that burlesque is intended. An actor playing the role might have provided a signal, just as an actress playing Amanda might have dismissed him with a facial expression suggesting that he need not despair. But within the printed text the relationship is decisively terminated—and Amanda can look forward only to celibacy within matrimony.

Sheridan takes over a phrase from Vanbrugh, 'Sure there's divinity about her,' (V.i.) but his Colonel Townly comes to a rapid determination to renew his pursuit of Berenthia. Sheridan, in other words, reduces the emotional intensity of the episode, he removes the ambiguity of it, and he brings it into a functional relationship with his principal action.

Sheridan's omission of Vanbrugh's opening scene presumably

derived from analogous motives—though in this instance Vanbrugh's intent seems more obviously parodic. The scene was needed in 1696 to establish continuity with *Love's Last Shift*; it was not needed in 1777 when parody of *Love's Last Shift* was not a consideration. As *The Relapse* opens, Loveless in his country house looks up from his reading to meditate, in soliloquy, on the quiet pleasures of rural retirement:

> How true is that Philosophy, which says,
> Our Heaven is seated in our Minds?
> Through all the Roving Pleasures of my Youth,
> (Where Nights and Days seem'd all consum'd in Joy,
> Where the false Face of Luxury
> Display'd such Charms,
> As might have shaken the most holy Hermit,
> And made him totter at his Altar;)
> I never knew one Moment's Peace like this.
> Here—in this little soft Retreat,
> My Thoughts unbent from all the Cares of Life,
> Content with Fortune,
> Eas'd from the grating Duties of Dependance,
> From Envy free, Ambition under foot,
> The raging Flame of wild destructive Lust
> Reduc'd to a warm pleasing Fire of lawful Love,
> My Life glides on, and all is well within.

Loveless may have reason to be satisfied with his new-found contentment, but scarcely shows any originality of mind. His praise of the independence and freedom from envy and ambition that a life of quiet contemplation in rural retirement can bring is commonplace in the extreme. Horace's 'Integer vitae scelerisque purus' is probably the most famous expression of Loveless' thoughts, and it may not be coincidence that Horace's ode, like this soliloquy, can be read as an exercise in irony. In any event, Loveless has scarcely completed his meditation when his wife enters and learns that he must go to London, a seat of temptation which she at once understands may lead him away from fidelity and contentment.

In his opening scene, Sheridan immediately settles to the exposition his audience needs to understand the intrigues that are to follow. His concern to establish a functional relationship between Vanbrugh's largely independent plot lines is apparent throughout all five acts. Why the change of locale to Scarborough? The residents of London could plausibly be brought there and the country seat of Sir Tunbelly Clumsey could plausibly be placed nearby: all characters, in other words, could be at approximately the same place at the same time and most of them could have some part in the two lines of intrigue—that of the two mismatched couples and that of Young Fashion to win his brother's intended bride—which in *The Relapse* coexist without touching until the end. Lord Foppington's outrageous attempt on Amanda provides sufficient motive for Loveless and Colonel Townly to aid Young Fashion in making Sir Tunbelly believe that he is his titled older brother. All the main characters can be brought to Sir Tunbelly's house to participate in the deception, without the need of a final scene in London, as in Vanbrugh, for tidying up the loose ends of plot.

Sheridan, in brief, gave closer attention than Vanbrugh to the unity of action as well as to the unities of time and place. He clarified the the moral structure by changes in plot as well as in language. He retained enough of the cynicism and sexual intrigue of the original for his vision of fashionable society to resemble that in the near-contemporary *School for Scandal*. Yet he removed Vanbrugh's boldest expressions and situations. The result may be an inferior play to the original—I think that it is—but Sheridan's is closer in didactic strategy, attention to the decorum of polite society, and structure to the conception of neo-classical comedy articulated by most of the dramatic critics of the seventeenth century.

Less than three months after they first presented *A Trip to Scarborough*, the Drury Lane Company, on 8 May 1777, presented *The School for Scandal*. The brevity of the interval between the plays merits notice. It suggests that Sheridan wrote *The School for Scandal* with the distinctive excellences of Restoration comedy fresh in mind. It suggests as well his fluency in writing (as in speaking) when he was sufficiently aroused to draw on all his powers. In *A Trip to Scarborough*, to be sure, he merely revised an earlier play; and in *The School for Scandal* he made use of fragmentary drafts for a comedy—or comedies[15]—on which he had long been working. Even so, the speed with which he wrote dialogue of commanding brilliance reminds us of the fluency and eloquence he revealed the following decade in the impeachment and trial of Warren Hastings.

G

Scarcely less than the adaptation from Vanbrugh, *The School for Scandal* illustrates the neoclassical interpretation of Aristotle's brief remarks about comedy, just as it illustrates Pope's famous definition in *An Essay on Criticism* of 'true wit'. A didactic play in its laughing and satirical rendering of the vice of scandalmongering, it focuses attention on a group of contemptible characters who illustrate the forms assumed by malicious hypocrisy. Its satirical target is as clearly defined as those in comedies of Molière, Ben Jonson, and Aristophanes, and the target represents the antithesis of the charity celebrated in the plot. The comedy is neatly unified thematically in its satirical review of a vice and exemplary display of a corollary virtue. If we are troubled by an insufficient causal relationship among the different plot lines, let us remember the structure of Jonson's comic masterpieces, in which thematic unity is more apparent than relationships among the successive episodes. Sheridan's separate plot lines of Lady Teazle's marital dissatisfaction and Charles's and Joseph's competitive courtship of Maria converge in Sir Peter's discovery of his wife in Joseph's study; and if the chatter of Lady Sneerwell's circle fails to advance the action, it provides information about the relationship between the brothers Surface and the Teazle family and conveys a sense of the moral environment in which they live. Even the unities of time and place are loosely observed, though in 1777, a decade after Samuel Johnson's famous assault on them in his Preface to Shakespeare, there were few critics who cared whether Sheridan's imagined action took more than twenty-four hours or whether his imagined locales in fashionable London were close together.

In an old tradition of comedy, many of the characters are personifications of folly and vice, representative of a variety of aberrations (having at least a remote resemblance to Jonsonian humors), which are epitomized in their names. Lady Sneerwell and Lady Teazle are types of the general nature that Imlac recommended to the young Prince Rasselas, and they are lineal descendants of Congreve's Mrs. Frail and Lady Wishfort. Not subtle studies in motive or emotion, they are broadly and even boisterously drawn renderings of the vices suggested by their names, embodiments of female aberrations. Sheridan departed from the social and even more the moral assumptions that control most Restoration comedy, but he followed Restoration tradition, if not in plot, then in characterization and in dialogue.

A plot summary of *The School for Scandal* is more misleading than summaries of plots usually are, for it will of necessity focus on the conventional and contrived—and 'sentimental'—aspects of the play. These aspects appear in the consecutive action, the rival courtships of the brothers Surface, which provides the supporting framework for the conversational scenes. If we knew only a plot summary, we would think we were in the presence of a hackneyed moral fable. Yet an experience of the play itself, whether in the study or the theatre, gives a different impression. The 'scandalous' conversations and the unexpected and embarrassing confrontations of characters are the principal determinants of our response, particularly in the theatre. It is an excessive emphasis on the fable at the expense of the dialogue, I think, that has led to the recent undervaluing of the play.[16]

The rivalry between the two brothers is not presented in isolation, nor is it, to an audience or a reader, the focus of interest. Although Charles is mentioned by other characters from the beginning, he does not appear until the third act. Joseph appears prominently from the first scene, but he is after all a member of Lady Sneerwell's circle, one whose conversation typifies the malignity and hypocrisy which are Sheridan's satirical targets. So also Lady Teazle (first on stage in the second act), although her matrimonial relations with Sir Peter, the guardian of Maria, belong schematically with the Surface rather than the slanderers' plot. In a full experience of the play, the satirical dialogue, and the sharply realized hypocrites who speak it, create the dominant impression. The rivalry for Maria—whose presence on stage is minimal for one who is the matrimonial prize—does indeed provide the framing action, with 'a beginning, middle, and end'. Yet if our sympathies are engaged on behalf of Charles and Maria, we leave a performance of the play, not with a benign pleasure in seeing benevolence rewarded, but rather with a disturbing recollection of malicious persons who embody ubiquitous qualities of mind as well as of heart.

Sheridan himself emphasizes the prominence, and by implication the priority, of the scandal scenes in his dedicatory poem to Mrs. Crew, forming his compliment to her on her immunity from the

> prim Adepts in Scandal's School
> Who rail by Precept, and Detract by rule.

This might have been a politic and necessary disclaimer in a poem addressed to a beautiful woman who was also a celebrated hostess. Yet

Garrick's prologue, which in its central paragraphs is an adroit imitation of the conversation of Lady Sneerwell's circle, has a similar focus. 'Thus at our friends we laugh,' Garrick writes—and the simple truth of the satirical burden of the play should not obscure its abiding relevance—

> who feel the Dart—
> To reach *our* feelings, we ourselves must Smart.

Like everything else about *The School for Scandal*, the prologue by Garrick and the epilogue by George Colman the Elder achieve an uncommon level of excellence; and within the idiom of their literary forms they suggest what Garrick and Colman considered to be Sheridan's accomplishments and limitations. In the epilogue '*Spoken by Mrs. Abington in the Character of Lady Teazle,*' Colman turns to the aspect of the play that is most vulnerable to criticism: Sheridan's failure to confront realistically the incompatibility of Sir Peter and Lady Teazle. Colman follows the familair convention of permitting a character to regret a repentance which promises dull domesticity:

> and yet I might deplore
> That the gay dream of dissipation's o'er;
> And say, ye fair, was ever lively Wife,
> Born with a genius for the highest Life
> Like me, untimely blasted in her bloom.
> Like me condemn'd to such a dismal doom?

Mrs. Abington, who less than three months before had played Miss Hoyden in *A Trip to Scarborough*, speaks with Miss Hoyden's lack of inhibition; and she speaks as well with Marjorie Pinchwife's and Mrs. Sullen's preference for the pleasures of the town over the dull routine of life in the country. Even before *The School for Scandal* was first performed, Colman saw the weakness of Sheridan's 'fable'.

Sheridan's depiction of Lady Teazle's repentance and Charles's triumph are alike vulnerable to the charges of those critics who find in the play an over-reliance on a benign and supervising providence to ensure the ultimate happiness of benevolent or reclaimable characters. Like other Georgian dramatists Sheridan assumes a sanctity in the marriage bond which inhibits an examination of sexual passion. All this is true, but it is far from the whole or even the principal truth about a play in which continuity of plot is so manifestly subordinate in dramatic interest to the satirical texture of the dialogue. Only if plot be isolated from what the characters say can a charge of 'triteness and triviality' be sustained. It is perhaps not irrelevant to recall Samuel Johnson's famous remark about the plot and the 'sentiments' of Richardson's *Clarissa*. *The School for Scandal* has a sustained quality of witty prose dialogue that only Dryden and Congreve equalled or surpassed in the late seventeenth century. In casual conversation Sheridan's characters—exemplifying envy, greed, ingratitude, detraction, malice—often rise to acute social and psychological insights. Few men living in the twentieth century would be willing to say that satire directed at scandalmongering and hypocrisy has become irrelevant.

Even in Sheridan's lifetime, there seems to have been differences of opinion about the relative importance of the gossip of Lady Sneerwell's circle and the rival courtship of Joseph and Charles Surface. Eight years after Sheridan's death, his niece, in a biography of her grandmother, wrote a rebuttal to criticism of the play made by John Watkins, Sheridan's early biographer. Watkins, after criticizing the play for its lack of a 'regular plot' or 'connected story,' remarked that even admirers of the play would find difficulty in praising its 'moral tendency'.[17] In answering Watkins, Sheridan's niece, Alicia Lefanu, acknowledged that the plot about the Surfaces is derivative and faulty: '. . . those who seek for morality in the character of Charles Surface, will be disappointed. . .'. They are looking in the wrong place, she argues: '. . . if they look for the moral tendency . . . in the proper place, it will be found to be excellent. . .'. Unlike the rival courtship of the Surfaces, which is conventional, the 'moral portion' is Sheridan's original creation 'and is conceived in a manner equally just, pointed, and forcible. It consists in a lively exposure of the effects of a baneful propensity, . . . a propensity to slander and detraction.'[18] This interpretation has the appearance of an expression of long-held family opinion. Alicia Lefanu refers to conversations with her mother, Sheridan's sister, about the origins of the play, and we may plausibly assume that they would have talked as well about praise and criticism of it they had heard and read. Although the interpretation is moralistic in terminology, it is nevertheless directed to the impact made by the play on the spectator or reader, and it is relevant to a consideration of Sheridan's plot and satire.

The plot and the satire can scarcely be separated except in exercises of literary analysis. Certainly the conversational sharpness is not confined to Lady Sneerwell's circle. Some of the most acerbic lines are spoken

between Sir Peter and Lady Teazle. The conversations of Lady Sneerwell and her friends are consistently brought into a functional relationship with the rivalry between the Surface brothers. Joseph and Lady
Teazle are members of the scandal circle. The idle banter of the circle
conveys not only Sheridan's thematic preoccupations but factual
information about Charles and Joseph. We cannot make the charge
about *The School for Scandal* that Dryden leveled at one of his own
plays: 'As to avoid a satire upon others, I will make bold with my
Marriage-a-la-Mode, where there are manifestly two actions, not
depending on one another. . .'.[19] Sheridan uses both the cautionary
method of dramatic satire and the exemplary method of moral fable—
but Molière had done the same thing. Molière had also, let us remember, rewarded virtuous characters and shown a reverence for marriage.

From the beginning critics recognized that the linguistic virtuosity of
Sheridan's characters, even more than the superbly contrived confrontations of characters, represented Sheridan's special achievement.
Writing in *The Morning Post*, 9 May 1777, the day after the first
performance, a reviewer noted that 'the principal excellence of the
Comedy will be found in the wit and elegance of the dialogue'; and
two centuries later not many modern students would disagree, though
many disagree in their final evaluations of the play. It is in his dialogue
that Sheridan most resembles the great comic dramatists of the late
seventeenth century. He knew, admired, and produced in his theatre the
plays of Congreve; and more nearly than anyone else in the eighteenth
century he approximated the stylistic accomplishment of *The Double-
Dealer*, *Love for Love*, and *The Way of the World*, in which the metaphorical texture of statement is often of more consequence than
primary meaning. Sheridan's characters, like Congreve's, strain for
epigram, and frequently they achieve it, in expressions so neatly turned
that a remark which is appropriate dramatically articulates a thought
that has occurred to many people at many times. 'I'm called away by
particular Business,' says Sir Peter, 'but I leave my Character behind
me,' (II.ii) and the thought, if not the phrase, has been in other minds
in comparable situations. The characters achieve their effects, not by
extravagance of conceit or unusual boldness of metaphor, but by
common images used in unexpected ways; and they make judgements
of unexpected acerbity. The dialogue resembles familiar conversation
in its separate components, but it is syntactically much more carefully
contrived than even the best conversation, and it scores its satirical

points with more regularity than the cleverest wit ever did in unpre-meditated repartee. The eighteenth-century fondness for elaboration of sentence structure, with frequent parallelism and antithesis, is apparent, and as we read the closely controlled prose we find it easy to under-stand why Samuel Johnson proposed Sheridan for membership in the Club.

Note Mrs. Candour's 'defence' of Miss Sallow against Crabtree's observation that she is an 'aukward Gawky without any one good Point under Heaven!' (II.ii):

> *Mrs. Candour:* Positively you shall not be so very severe. Miss Sallow is a Relation of mine by marriage and as for her Person great allowance is to be made—for let me tell you a woman labours under many disadvantages who tries to pass for a girl at six and thirty.

The length of the second sentence and its clarity despite the syntactical complexity exemplify Sheridan's unobtrusive skill in stylistic reinforce-ment of his characters' self-revelation of hypocritical malice. The length and structure of the sentence suggest as well the stern demands Sheridan makes of actors and actresses, with regard to pauses for breath, in pacing his dialogue. After Lady Sneerwell responds am-biguously to the criticism of Miss Sallow, Mrs. Candour replies in her distinctive idiom of detraction masquerading as praise: '. . . and then as to her manner—upon my word I think it is particularly graceful considering she never had the least Education for you know her Mother was a Welch milliner and her Father a Sugar-Baker at Bristol.' This is the dialogue of a stylist who is also an anatomist of conversa-tional malice.

We could object to Sheridan's dialogue, as critics have objected to Congreve's, on the grounds that it is too consistently witty to function effectively as a means of characterization. Not always, of course: Mrs. Candour's lines, like her name, define her character. Such differentia-tion as exists in conversational ability is to the advantage of the malicious and hypocritical, for they enjoy the more uninhibited use of their faculties. Unlike Congreve, who gives a conversational advantage to his true wits, Sheridan shows the superior merits of his sympathetic characters by their deeds. His play does not (and here it differs from *The Way of the World*) convey a reverence for good conversation as one of the highest arts of civilization.

It may aid us to avoid an overemphasis on the defects in Sheridan's plot to recall that the single Restoration comedy which most closely anticipates Sheridan's preoccupation with slander is Wycherley's *The Plain Dealer*, in which satirical dialogue is carried by a plot little short of the absurd. The more frequent comparison of *The School for Scandal* to *The Way of the World* rather than to *The Plain Dealer* derives from the resemblance of Congreve and Sheridan in wit dialogue and in pre-occupation with 'reputation'. But in his unceasing exposure of malicious gossip, Sheridan is closer to Wycherley. James Boaden assumed that Sheridan had taken his central idea from *The Plain Dealer*: Sheridan, Boaden wrote, followed *A Trip to Scarborough* 'on the 8th of May by that brilliant effusion, which placed the *School for Scandal* before the Plain Dealer, which suggested it, and surpassed in *stage effect*, while it at least equalled in *wit*, the Double Dealer of Congreve.'[20] Apart from Boaden's statement, I know of no reason, except the thematic similarity between the two plays, to assume that Sheridan planned *The School for Scandal* with *The Plain Dealer* in mind.[21] Yet the fact Boaden thought that he had done so, as well as Boaden's choice of the most bitter of Congreve's comedies, *The Double-Dealer*, to bring into the comparisons, implies that he regarded *The School for Scandal*, not as a bland and 'sentimental' dramatic fable, but rather as a pungent dramatic satire directed against the cruel small talk of fashionable London.

Wycherley is immune to the charges of disguised sentimentalism that are directed against Sheridan. His satirical vision in *The Plain Dealer* is darker than Sheridan's, his railing review of English society a closer approximation, in method and tone, to the non-dramatic satire of the Renaissance[22] than anything in Sheridan. Yet *The School for Scandal* and *The Plain Dealer* are alike in the primacy accorded conversational exposure of vice at the expense of plot. The plot of *The Plain Dealer* is more loosely contrived, more disjointed in its separate episodes, and less credible than that of *The School for Scandal*. We need only recall Fidelia's role to be reminded of the impression of hurried improvisation conveyed by the plot (which is strikingly different in this regard from the neatly structured *Country Wife*). Like Sheridan in *The School for Scandal*, Wycherley in *The Plain Dealer* (the second act of which is similar to Sheridan's scenes in Lady Sneerwell's lodgings) lavished his attention on his characters' talk rather than their intrigues.

When Sir Fretful Plagiary in *The Critic* expresses a fear that the

proprietor of Drury Lane—that is, Sheridan—will steal hints from a
tragedy for use in a comedy, Sheridan laughingly conveys an objection
to the confounding of dramatic genres but he also recalls charges made
against himself that he had taken over the literary property of other
persons. Perhaps he had in mind such absurd stories as that reported by
John Watkins[23]—and decisively refuted by Sheridan's niece[24]—that
Sheridan had appropriated the manuscript of *The School for Scandal*,
which had been written by 'a young lady, the daughter of a merchant
in Thames Street. . .'. Although more implausible than most such
stories, this one belongs to a genre of accusations to which author-
managers, among them Cibber and Garrick, were vulnerable. Yet in
Sir Fretful Plagiary's remark, Sheridan may also have had in mind more
generalized charges that in *The School for Scandal* he had 'borrowed'
from earlier writers. Like most other dramatists, Sheridan had indeed
drawn freely from literary tradition.

How firmly *The School for Scandal*, its resemblances to Wycherley,
Vanbrugh, and Congreve notwithstanding, derives from Georgian
comic tradition may be illustrated by comparing it with Arthur
Murphy's *Know Your Own Mind*. So closely does *The School for
Scandal* resemble Murphy's play, first performed in February 1777, just
three months before Sheridan's in May, that had the sequence been
reversed we would be inclined to regard *Know Your Own Mind* as
imitative and derivative.[25] We are not so inclined to regard *The
School for Scandal*, and for good reason even apart from its excellence.
Sheridan had been at work on *The School for Scandal* for a long time,
writing and rewriting dialogue, and combining plot lines that may have
been intended originally for separate plays. He succeeded triumphantly
in producing a play that in the quality of its dialogue bears his own
mark—the sensitive prose style that would soon make him a famous
orator. We cannot say with assurance that he took nothing from
Murphy's *Know Your Own Mind*, but he could not have taken much
from it. Yet the appearance in a single season of two such similar plays,
written independently of one another, is no accident. It is a result of the
inescapable force of the shared assumptions and ideals that constitute
tradition. The two dramatists were at one in admiring and attempting
to emulate the wit of Restoration comedy even as they accepted the
inhibitions and moral premises of their own time.

Even more overtly than *The School for Scandal*, Murphy's play recalls *The Way of the World*. One of the principal characters has a name Millamour, which is a masculine rendering of that of Congreve's famous heroine; another character, a widow of uncertain age, Mrs. Bromley, resembles Lady Wishfort in more than her use of face paint. She too is a rival of her own niece for a young man who loves the niece, and she too is deceived by a scheming young man. Even more than Sheridan's characters, Murphy's correspond to the Restoration categories of true wits and would-be wits. Millamour and Dashwood are true wits, and so is Lady Bell, as close an approximation of Millamant as Murphy could make her—and a successful approximation, described by a critic writing in *The Morning Post*, 24 February 1777, as 'one of the most perfact and natural female characters we have seen on the stage for many years'. Although a more genial rendering of the character type, Sir Harry Lovewit resembles Congreve's Witwoud. A contrasting couple of more serious lovers, not present in *The Way of the World* but frequently appearing in other Restoration comedies, re-appear in Lady Jane and Captain Bygrove. Murphy's plot is almost as complicated as Congreve's, and he too focuses attention on trials of conversational wit that take the hypocrisies of London society as their subject.

In its satirical dimension the play anticipates *The School for Scandal* just as it resembles *The Way of the World*. Mr. Bygrove's response to Malvil's invitation to leave the company (III)—'No, Sir, I shall not leave the enemy in this room behind me: a bad translator of an ancient poet,' he says about Dashwood, 'is not so sure to deface his original, as his licentious strain to disparage every character'—resembles in intent though it is less concise Sir Peter Teazle's remark in a similar situation. In *Know Your Own Mind* as in *The School for Scandal* the courtships are carried on against a choral background of scandalmongering and in opposition to the intrigues of the malicious. And one of the malicious characters, Malvil, resembles Joseph Surface in personality as also in his role in the play.

Like the elder Surface, Malvil disguises his perfidy beneath a veneer of sensibility. 'To a person of sentiment, like you, madam,' Malvil says to the widow Mrs. Bromley, 'a visit is paid with pleasure.' Mrs. Bromley echoes his praise of good nature. 'I admire your sensibility, Mr. Bygrove,' she replies (II.i), just before she directs a verbal assault against her dependent relative, Miss Neville. To Murphy as to Sheridan 'sentiment' and 'sensibility' were the cant terms of hypocrites, the verbal camouflage of malice. Malvil's treachery is more malignant than Joseph Surface's in the proportion that planned rape of a defenceless girl is worse than the attempted seduction of a married woman. The exposure of his treachery, in a situation analogous though less well contrived than the screen scene, approaches the melodramatic as *The School for Scandal* never does.

Know Your Own Mind was warmly received in February 1777, and perhaps it would have been more successful later had *The School for Scandal* not appeared in May. A critic writing in *The Morning Post*, 24 February 1777, calls it 'the production of a dramatic writer of no inconsiderable genius'. He praises the dialogue as 'every way superior to that which we meet with in our modern comedies; discovering veins of wit and humour, that would do no disgrace to the literary reputation of those writers, who hold the first rank in our drama'. He refers to the 'admirable diversification' of the characters and the 'fine contrasts' among them, though he remarks on their lack of originality.

Know Your Own Mind represents as close an approach as we will find in Georgain comedy, Goldsmith's plays not excepted, to Sheridan's best play. Yet it does not approximate *The School for Scandal* in quality. It loses focus by reason of its amplitude, encompassing as it does the affairs of some four different couples. The dialogue is inferior to Sheridan's but it is more than merely competent. Murphy's play deserves more reputation than it has, and if it were better known today there would be less inclination to regard *The School for Scandal* as an isolated phenomenon.

William Hazlitt, in his *Lectures on the English Comic Writers*, assumes that Sheridan drew from *Know Your Own Mind* in writing *The School for Scandal*. 'It is hard that the fate of plagiarism should attend upon originality:' Hazlitt remarked, 'yet it is clear that the elements of the School for Scandal are not sparingly scattered in Murphy's comedy of Know your own Mind, which appeared before the latter play, only to be eclipsed by it.' And Hazlitt cites resemblances of detail between the plays, including the similarity of Murphy's Malvil and Joseph Surface; but he does so, not to convict Sheridan of plagiarism, but rather to explain the manner in which Sheridan, by his clarity of focus on the significant detail, surpasses Murphy. Hazlitt wrote before the publication in 1825 of Thomas Moore's biography of Sheridan, in which Moore prints preliminary drafts of dialogue that in revised form appear in *The School for Scandal*. These drafts[26] as well as the testimony of

Sheridan's sister[27] leave little doubt that the play was essentially original and that Sheridan had worked on it over a prolonged period of time. Yet remembering that he completed it in haste and that he had an extraordinarily retentive memory, I think it not impossible that he took suggestions—perhaps without knowing that he was doing so—from *Know Your Own Mind*. Some details seem too close to one another to be the result of coincidence.

Sheridan's preliminary drafts reveal a slow and even laborious evolution of the play, of movement from collected scraps of 'scandalous' dialogue to the two distinct components of the play, the one with a focus on Lady Sneerwell's circle and the other on the affairs of Sir Peter Teazle's family. Thomas Moore thought that these two components were first intended for separate plays.[28] Cecil Price, however, reports that he is 'not altogether convinced' that Sheridan had planned to use the fragments in separate plays—and Price supports his doubts with an analysis of features common to both the embryonic plots.[29] In any event, the early drafts reveal Sheridan collecting and relishing phrases, much as Swift did in compiling his *Complete Collection of Genteel and Ingenious Conversation*, though with the difference that Swift searched for banality and Sheridan for malice. All we know about the composition of *The School for Scandal* (and indeed about its publication)[30] suggests a kind of stylistic perfectionism.

The depiction in *The School for Scandal* of a benevolent man's triumph over a hypocrite illustrates a homely moral truth that was popular in the eighteenth century. So also was the story that is its vehicle in the comedy: that of two rivals, the one dissolute but possessing the redeeming gift of charity and the other superficially decorous but in fact malignant, competing for a prize which is love and a fortune. *Tom Jones* is the most famous version of it, and in Fielding's novel as in Sheridan's play there is a paradoxical but indispensable sophistication of manner in the telling of the tale.

The resemblance of the play to the novel is inescapable. It was noted in *The Morning Chronicle* as early as 9 May 1777:

> The two principal [characters], Joseph and Charles Surface, are the Blifil and Tom Jones of the piece.—The first a man of great morality and most refined sentiment, from the teeth outwards, but at heart a mean, mercenary, malignant villain. The second a gay, dissipated rake, apparently a slave to fashionable folly, and

a dupe to extravagance and profligacy, but in truth an honest, open, generous fellow, whose heart is ever melted at a tale of distress, and whose purse, while it holds a guinea, is ever open to the wants of the miserable and unfortunate.

Charles, in other words, is a man of feeling, one of many in eighteenth-century literature, of whom Tom Jones is but the most widely known. The resemblance of the play to the novel does not in fact extend far beyond the contrasted characters of the brothers and their rivalry in love. It has been suggested that the screen scene may have originated in Sheridan's recollection of the episode in *Tom Jones* in which Tom, talking to the pregnant Molly Seagrim in her own room, suddenly sees Mr. Square when the rug behind which he has been hiding falls.[31] Perhaps, but this is a subject for speculation. Yet the resemblance of the novel and the play can help us to a just esteem for *The School for Scandal* if for no other reason than that the high reputation of *Tom Jones* provides aid in defending Sheridan against criticism of his authorial evaluation of characters and manipulation of plot to favour the benevolent and virtuous.

Again we are driven to that inescapable adjective 'sentimental'. The word is used ironically in *The School for Scandal* to convey the hypocritical fondness of Joseph for moralistic platitudes. Of sentimentalism in the pejorative sense, implying a wilful exploitation of emotion, Sheridan is singularly free, and in fact the play is remarkable for the contrary qualities of sustained gaiety and satirical astringency. We need not belabour the meaning of a frequently misused word and argue, in opposition to Sheridan's manifest intention, that the play is indeed 'sentimental'. Yet the ethical assumptions controlling the implied evaluations of his characters are largely those responsible for the sentimental movement in eighteenth-century literature. Sheridan is at one with the sentimentalists in focusing attention on episodes that illustrate the presence or absence of benevolence in his characters. Like Sterne and Goldsmith he has the redeeming gifts of style, wit, and intelligence, but also like them—in *A Sentimental Journey* and *The Vicar of Wakefield*—he explores the principal theme of the writers we consider to be sentimentalists: the emotional responsiveness of some if not all men to the distresses of others. This perhaps is merely to say that Sheridan, however determined not to be overemphatic or clumsy in depicting situations of emotional intensity, was a man of his times, responding to human relationships like other writers of the later eighteenth century and in a very different manner from that in which Congreve responded to them at the end of the seventeenth century.

Sheridan is tolerant of deviations from prudent behaviour as the seventeenth-century dramatists were not. In the marriage of Sir Peter and Lady Teazle, we encounter a relationship—an elderly but rich man married to a beautiful young woman who had accepted him to escape an obscure and impoverished life—that is reminiscent of earlier comedy. It has some similarity to the relationship between Mr. Fondlewife and Laetitia in Congreve's *The Old Bachelor* or even to that between Mr. Pinchwife and Margery in Wycherley's *The Country Wife*. The change in Lady Teazle, from quiet country girl before marriage to imperious gossip afterwards, reminds us of the change in 'the silent woman' of Jonson's *Epicene*; and the rapidity with which Lady Teazle acquires the skills of a coquette recalls the education of Agnès, Arnolphe's intended wife in Molière's *L'École des femmes*. Unlike Sheridan, the seventeenth-century dramatists were uniformly severe in their satirical handling of an old man's folly in aspiring to marriage with a young girl. Sir Peter seems destined for the cuckoldry that actually befalls Fondlewife and Pinchwife. Yet the event is otherwise, and it is a measure of the distance between Sheridan and the earlier comedy.

To be sure, Sheridan provides early in the play (II.ii) a forewarning that Lady Teazle has not altogether lost the moral principles that guided her youth in the country. When Joseph Surface asks her, in an idiom of male libertinism that has changed little in two hundred years, when she is to give him, as she has promised, her opinion of his library, she replies with unexpected force:

> No—no I begin to think it would be imprudent—and you know
> I admit you as a Lover no further than Fashion requires.—
> *Surface.* True—a mere Platonic Cicisbeo—what every London
> wife is entitled too.
> *Lady Tezale.* Certainly one must not be out of the Fashion—
> however I have so much of my country Prejudices left—
> that—tho' Sir Peter's ill humour may vex me ever so— it
> shall never provoke me to—
> *Surface.* The only revenge in your Power—well I applaud your
> moderation.
> *Lady Teazle.* Go—you are an insinuating Wretch—

Yet Lady Teazle later consents to visit Joseph's library—and the result is the famous 'screen scene' (IV.iii). She explains to Joseph that Sir Peter has become jealous of Charles (and Joseph in an aside expresses pleasure that his 'scandalous Friends keep that up—'). Lady Teazle has reached the dangerous conclusion that if her husband suspects her 'without cause, it follows that the best way of curing his Jealousy is to give him reason for 't'.

Saved by accident from compromising herself, she overhears Sir Peter explaining the generous provisions he has made for her financial security; and like many another character of the eighteenth-century sentimental tradition she is brought by this experience of magnanimity to an understanding of her folly and to a resolution to amend her conduct. Sheridan's difference from Congreve and Wycherley is partly a matter of increased restraint in portraying sexual relationships. But more is involved; above all, a greater tolerance and kindliness in handling aberrations from prudent and rational norms of conduct.[32] Despite the matrimonial harmony established between Sir Peter and Lady Teazle at the end of the play, they remain a couple ill-matched in age and temperament. Sir Peter's initial indiscretion in marrying a very much younger woman is not and cannot be remedied; it is merely forgiven, and we are implicitly asked to believe that it no longer matters greatly. Sheridan indeed treats Sir Peter as a kind of later Sir Roger de Coverley, in whom folly and imperceptiveness become endearing qualities because they are consequences of emotional spontaneity.

Yet notwithstanding the indulgence shown to Sir Peter in his marriage—and to Charles Surface in his improvidence and dissipation —the tone of the play is, as I have said, acerbic. The scandal scenes recur like a thematic refrain. Sheridan's indignation at calculated scandalmongering, especially the published kind appearing in such journals as *The Town and Country Magazine* mentioned by Snake, gives timeliness to his social satire. The neatly turned epigrams, in which malice is bearable because it is clever, establish the milieu in which the characters live out their lives. The malice of the gossips in *The School for Scandal* poses questions concerning human benevolence. And so, by way of a contrast between the scandalmongers and the men of good will, there is established the distinctive tone of the play, that balance between sentiment and satire typical of the Age of Johnson at its best.

The initial run of *The School for Scandal* was a triumph. Audiences as

well as critics were delighted, and from the first performance on 8 May
until the end of the theatrical season in early June, the comedy drew full
houses. For several years receipts from it were consistently higher than
for other plays. In 1779 the Treasurer of the company noted that it had
'damped the new pieces'.[33] 'No modern theatrical piece ever met with
a fuller success, nor deserved it more,' a critic wrote about *The School for
Scandal* in *The Gazetteer*, 9 May 1777, 'which was performed last
night . . . for the first time. It is a production of Mr. Sheridan, junior,
who seems to have inherited the exalted genius of both Congreve and
Vanbrugh, and bids fair to revive the fallen glory of the British drama.'
A critic for *The Morning Post* wrote the same day that it was more
'universally and deservedly well received' than any other comedy he
could remember. As we would expect the reviewers praised the quality
of the dialogue and the adroit contrivance of the screen scene. 'There
hardly ever was a better dramatic situation than that which occurs in
the fourth act,' wrote the critic for *The Morning Chronicle*, 9 May,
'where Sir Peter discovers Lady Teazle in Joseph Surface's study.' The
dialogue, he remarked, 'is easy, engaging, and witty'. With some
variation in adjectives, the other reviewers said much the same thing,
though with occasional qualifications, as in the comment of *The
Morning Post*, 9 May, that some of the '*wit traps*' in the second act seem
too studiously contrived. There are other critical notes, such as the
comment in *The Morning Chronicle*, 9 May, that 'the satire upon the
score of scandal is rather overcharged, and the last act appears to have
been hastily made up'. But the tenor of the reviews could scarcely have
been more laudatory if Sheridan had written them himself.

Sheridan had known and taken into account as he wrote the special
abilities of the actors and actresses, with the result that there was an
unusual harmony between an individual's skills and the demands of his
role. Horace Walpole said that more parts were well acted in it than in
any other play he could remember.[34] Three years later Walpole
commented indirectly on the lesser impact of the play in the study than
on the stage. 'Apropos to the theatre,' he wrote in a letter to William
Mason, 19 May 1780, 'I have *read* the *School for Scandal*: it is rapid and
lively, but is far from containing the wit I expected from seeing it
acted.'[35] Sheridan was well served by the company at Drury Lane. Only
Priscilla Hopkins as Maria in the play's first run seems to have been
disappointing; and it is worth noting that Sheridan had not originally
intended her for the role.[36]

James Boaden, who in 1825 included in his biography of John Philip Kemble 'A History of the Stage, from the Time of Garrick to the Present Period,' describes the professional styles of Sheridan's actors. His account of William Smith, who played Charles Surface, and of Robert Palmer, who played Joseph, suggests their suitability for their roles. Acknowledging that Smith's 'articulation was not nice,' Boaden reports that in appearance Smith 'was fair and noble'. 'His deportment was dignified and manly—his action graceful, and never redundant.'[37] He had qualities, we may conclude, that would have made him more successful as a 'man of feeling' than as a 'man of wit'. Boaden's account of Palmer suggests his suitability for the role of the hypocritical and pompous Joseph. Noting that in comedy Palmer gave the impression of having attained the qualities of a fine gentleman rather than of having been born to them, Boaden writes that he 'had a sort of elaborate grace and stately superiority, which he affected on all occasions. . .'.[38] Boaden describes Thomas King in the role of Sir Peter Teazle: 'Nothing approached him in the dry and timid habitual bachelor, drawn into the desperate union with youth and beauty and gaiety. His Sir Peter Teazle was a master-piece.'[39]

The character offering the widest range of interpretations is surely Lady Teazle, first played by Mrs. Abington.[40] She, as the facts about her early life plainly imply, was a country gentlewoman with a veneer of recently acquired sophistication. Sir Peter in soliloquy (I.ii) describes her former life. He had chosen her with caution, he says—

a Girl bred whol[l]y in the country—who never knew Luxury beyond one silk Gown nor Dissipation above the annual Gala of a Race-Ball—yet now she plays her Part in all the extravagant Fopperies of the Fashion and the Town, with as ready a Grace as if she had never seen a Bush nor a grass plat out of Grosvenor-Square—!

All this change in a mere six months of marriage! The fact that Sheridan wrote (or at least completed) the part for Mrs. Abington, who had recently excelled as Miss Hoyden in his *A Trip to Scarborough*, would seem to imply that he intended in the character a subdued comment on the rapidity with which a country girl could acquire town vices. Boaden's praise of Mrs. Abington's versatility suggests that she could have conveyed an ambiguity of status in London society: 'Mrs. Abington seemed to combine in her excellence the requisites for both the fashionable lady and her maid, and more, much more, than all this. She was the most brilliant satirist of her sex.'[41] Yet apart from Sir Peter's and Lady Teazle's several references to her impoverished youth and Joseph Surface's reference to the 'ill effects' of her education in the country (IV.iii), Sheridan included little in dialogue to convey a tension between her past life and her present surroundings and aspirations. Unlike Marjorie Pinchwife in Wycherley's play, Lady Teazle uses no rustic phrases that would reveal her earlier life. The inhibitions which—aided by coincidence—save her from Joseph Surface's blandishments might be attributed to a youth spent at a remove from London society, though residence in the country produced no such results in Majorie Pinchwife or Miss Hoyden. In any event, her inhibitions do not prevent her from accepting an invitation to visit privately the library of a man who has already made advances to her. If a tension in Lady Teazle's personality was to be revealed to an audience, the actress herself had the responsibility for doing so—and apparently Mrs. Abington, unlike her successor in the role, Miss Dorothy Jordan, chose not to do so.[42]

We must take *The School for Scandal* for what it is, not prejudging it by what other dramatists before and after Sheridan wrote or failed to write. Sheridan was not innovative. He did not anticipate the age which followed his own in exploring the recesses of the human personality. His characters lack subtlety of emotion and motivation. Yet he uses them with a superb sense of theatrical effect, and he gives them lines that, in concision and profundity of insight into social relationships, not infrequently recall Dryden, his favourite poet, and Pope. If a dramatic era ended with his comedies, it ended with a brilliance not unworthy of its beginning. It ended as well with comedies approximating 'neoclassical regularity' more fully than had Dryden's comedies of the 1660s.

5

The Theatre-Manager
and *The Critic*

Two and a half years after *The School for Scandal,* Drury Lane produced
as an afterpiece *The Critic,* Sheridan's final important play, a theatrical
burlesque in a distinguished tradition of English drama. Even more than
earlier theatrical burlesques, Sheridan's is an ironical statement of
dramatic ideals, and it is a personal statement. The most illuminating
antecedent of *The Critic* is perhaps to be found in non-dramatic
literature, in Pope's *Epistle to Dr. Arbuthnot.* Like the poem, the play is
a famous and influential writer's satirical commentary on the difficulties
of his position, including a defense of himself against detractors, and it
is an exposition of his convictions about his art.

The *Critic* has an advantage over earlier theatrical burlesques in its
prefatory first act, as sharply conceived in its satirical characterization
and its dialogue as *The School for Scandal.* Sheridan regarded this act,
justly I believe, as the best of his writing for the theatre.[1] If his first act
is less consistently autobiographical than Pope's *Arbuthnot,* it makes
overt references to Sheridan himself and his recent theatrical enter-
prises; and it includes in Mr. Dangle, Mr. Puff, and Sir Fretful Plagiary
caricatures of theatrical personalities who complicated Sheridan's life.
He satirized them, and yet he included in his characterization of them
humorous if intermittent glances at himself. Like Mr. Puff he had become a master in the art of self-advertisement. Like Sir Fretful he was
sensitive to criticism of his plays. Indeed, from the existence of *The
Critic,* we could guess that he was sensitive even without the testimony
provided by a man who knew him.[2] Far indeed from acknowledging
the literary crime of plagiarism, of which Sir Fretful in his surname

stands accused, Sheridan nevertheless acknowledges that he had been charged with it, even as he laughs at the charges. 'Besides—', Sir Fretful tells Sneer, 'I can tell you it is not always so safe to leave a play in the hands of those who write themeslves [I.i].'[3] In Mr. Dangle's remark about the fastidiousness of the audience, 'No double-entendre, no smart innuendo admitted; even Vanbrugh and Congreve obliged to undergo a bungling reformation! [I.i]', Sheridan glances at his own first season as proprietor of Drury Lane. We can easily imagine Elizabeth Sheridan expostulating to her husband, in the vein of Mrs. Dangle, about his preoccupation with the theatre. Mrs. Dangle, despite her irritation at her husband's obsession with the theatre, abides him and even helps him by reading manuscripts of plays, as Mrs. Sheridan did.

In the brief episode in which the Italian singers with their French interpreter appear in Mr. Dangle's drawing room [I.ii], Sheridan draws from his recent experience as part owner of the King's Theatre, which served as London's opera house. Together with Thomas Harris, proprietor of Covent Garden, Sheridan bought the King's Theatre in February 1778, and produced operas there starting in the autumn of that year. The venture was not successful financially, and, Harris having earlier withdrawn from it, Sheridan sold out in November 1781.[4] The proprietorship of the opera house was costly and no doubt troublesome to Sheridan; in 1779 he had reason enough to make a joke about Italian singers. Hence the seemingly gratuitous introduction of them and their incompetent French interpreter in *The Critic*, which otherwise, in its satirical dimension, is preoccupied with the kind of entertainment provided by Drury Lane and Covent Garden. To be sure, the appearance of the singers provides an occasion for songs, a sufficient reason for their presence; but the episode, coming mid-way in an act devoted to theatrical affairs as Sheridan had experienced them, should be interpreted, I think, as a comment on his proprietorship of the King's Theatre. A remark by Mrs. Dangle (I.i) sounds like a self-mocking description of the Sheridan household: 'And what is worse than all,' Mrs. Dangle says (after complaining that her drawing room had become 'an absolute register-office for candidate actors, and poets without character,') 'now that the Manager has monopoliz'd the Opera-House, haven't we the Signors and Signoras calling here, sliding their smooth semibreves, and gargling glib divisions in their outlandish throats. . . .'

Sheridan's pugnacity—again a quality reminiscent of Pope in *An Epistle to Dr. Arbuthnot*—is tempered in his first act by his ability to turn a clever phrase; but his wit notwithstanding, he writes defensively, employing caricature to settle old scores. Like Pope, he had a bill of complaints to settle. Together with his father and his wife, he had long suffered ridicule; and his sensitivity to it could scarcely have been lessened by his rapid rise in London society, which was a family-proud society to which Sheridan and his wife had no claim to belong except the considerable one of their own talents.[5] His father's irascibility as well as his profession of actor and teacher of elocution made him an easy target for ridicule. Thomas Sheridan as well as his daughter-in-law Elizabeth had provided subjects for Samuel Foote's dramatic caricatures. Since the duels with Thomas Mathews, Sheridan had provided the newspapers with good copy; and since the first performance of *The Rivals* he had been a target for the theatrical critics, who had not been unanimous in praise of his plays nor, after September 1776, his management of Drury Lane.[6] It is not coincidence that in *The School for Scandal* as well as in *The Critic* Sheridan strikes back at journalists.

The resemblances, stylistic as well as thematic, between the first acts of *The Critic* and *The School for Scandal* merit attention. There would be less misunderstanding and less underevaluation of the earlier, full-length comedy if all readers and audiences perceived that Sheridan's conception of his gossipmongering characters and their manner of speaking approximates that of burlesque, just as in *The Critic*. *The Rivals* and *The Duenna* reveal, in parody and caricature, the mode of burlesque as well, but they are less vulnerable to misinterpretation than *The School for Scandal* because, in their lesser subtlety, they are more openly renderings of traditional characters and comic situations. In attempting and achieving more in *The School for Scandal*, Sheridan ventured into ambiguities of tone with bitterness intruding into the gaiety to which he had previously limited himself. The bitterness reappears in the first act of *The Critic*, an act that follows conventions of the comedy of manners as that sub-genre had reached definition in Wycherley and Congreve. The second act of *The Plain Dealer*, consisting of a conversational review dominated by malicious hypocrites of the preoccupations of the fashionable, anticipates much that is distinctive about *The Critic*. Sheridan's mode of characterization is his own, but his satirical targets are familiar ones—and many of them can be described as personifications of malicious hypocrisy. Sneer provides an inventory of Sir Fretful Plagiary's vices, after a servant has announced Sir Fretful's arrival and before he makes his entrance (I.i), that is in the pattern of, though it is more comprehensive than, corresponding inventories in *The School for Scandal*. Mr. Dangle's acquiescence, with the qualifying refrain 'Tho' he's my friend', in Sneer's voluble account of Sir Fretful, puts us in mind of Pope's allusion in *An Epistle to Dr. Arbuthnot* to Addison's ability to 'hint a fault, and hesitate dislike.' Sneer's baiting of Sir Fretful after he appears reveals a virtuosity in malice to which Snake in the earlier play may aspire but scarcely reach.

The dialogue of the first act of *The Critic* has the clarity and precision of diction and syntax present throughout *The School for Scandal*. Unlike the parodic blank verse of Mr. Puff's 'Spanish Armada,' the conversation of Mr. Dangle and his friends is largely free of metaphorical language. The satirical hits come rapidly, but their force derives from the juxtaposition of ideas—as in Sneer's reference to a comedy about burglary—or from the juxtaposition of language and situation—as in Sir Fretful's brave attempt at indifference during Sneer's fabricated report of a newspaper review. Sheridan's verbal and situational irony is pervasive, and so is his allusiveness to types of persons connected with the theatre, to aberrations in the taste of dramatists and audiences alike, and to practices—such as the art of puffery—employed to give an undeserved popularity to plays. The first act is as allusive as the second and third acts, but with the difference that references to living persons are more prominent and references to actual plays less prominent.

Sheridan conveys his convictions about dramatic theory ironically in act one no less than in acts two and three, but with the difference that in the first he is mainly preoccupied with comedy and in the two later with tragedy. Mr. Dangle's reception of his friends provides a glimpse of problems of theatrical management arising from the clash of ambitious and egotistic persons engaged in an intensely competitive occupation. The conversation at Mr. Dangle's house includes observations about the nature of comedy. When Sir Fretful Plagiary expresses a fear that the proprietor of Drury Lane—that is, Sheridan—will steal hints from a tragedy for use in a comedy, Sheridan laughingly recalls charges made against himself but he also conveys an objection to the confounding of dramatic genres. Sneer's reference to a new comedy called *The Reformed Housebreaker*, written by one of his friends 'who has discovered that the follies and foibles of society, are subjects unworthy the notice of the Comic Muse, who should be taught to stoop only at the greater vices and blacker crimes of humanity,' is a sufficiently blunt protest, by the author of *The School for Scandal*, against the introduction of tragic or potentially tragic subjects into comedy.

It is easy to find recent plays that might have prompted Sheridan's protest. Cumberland's *The Fashionable Lover* of 1772, for example, depicts a virtuous heroine whose distresses, before the denouement of the fifth act, have more than a casual resemblance to those of Clarissa Harlowe in the first half of Richardson's novel. She is the victim of embezzlement as well as of attempted rape. Colman's *The Suicide* of 1778 employs as a principal episode in comedy an attempted suicide, thwarted when the desperate young man's fiancée substitutes a sleeping potion for poison. Sheridan includes ironical criticism as well of the preference shown by some dramatists for the exemplary over the satirical or cautionary method of conveying instruction. Sneer's echo of a summary remark by a character in Kelly's *False Delicacy* of 1768, that 'the theatre, in proper hands, might certainly be made of the school of morality,' may be taken as an objection to a theory of comedy made popular by Steele early in the century.[7] Kelly's play, its ironic comment on excessive 'delicacy' notwithstanding, provides almost as insistently as Steele's *The Conscious Lovers* models of exemplary conduct. Sheridan is scarcely less pugnacious than Pope in *An Epistle to Dr. Arbuthnot*, and he is as ready to identify his targets. But he was writing satire rather than a judicious survey of Georgian drama. Almost all the ironic points he made had been anticipated by his older contemporaries.

Stage burlesques, often in the form of mock rehearsals, had been popular since the Renaissance. They are important for historians of the theatre and drama. They represent drama at its most self-conscious, preoccupied with the relationship between the art of the theatre—to which the dramatist, the director, the scene designer, and the actor, among others, contribute—and the illusion produced in the minds of the audience. They are drama's mirror of itself. At their best, they confront drama in its epistemological dimension, either overtly, as in Pirandello's *Six Characters in Search of an Author*, or by implication, as in Beaumont's *Knight of the Burning Pestle*. In the latter play, actions at different removes from the life of the audience occur together. The naïve misunderstanding of the grocer's wife of the nature of theatrical illusion compels us to recognize the habits of mind needed for the comprehension of drama.[8]

Not precisely a stage 'rehearsal', *The Knight of the Burning Pestle* nevertheless includes, in the apprentice's intrusion into the play being performed, impromptu adventures which elicit comment from spectators. Interaction between actors and audience is frequent in stage burlesques. Beaumont's Induction, though far briefer than Sheridan's first act, resembles it in the characters' conversation about theatrical affairs before the play to be acted begins. That *The Knight of the Burning Pestle* provides more information about stage and dramatic history than *The Critic* is a consequence not so much of differences between the plays as of the fact that in the eighteenth century alternative sources of information are far more plentiful. To read Herbert S. Murch's comprehensive introduction to Beaumont's play is to become aware that the play provides a satirical record of popular drama that has largely disappeared.[9] Sheridan's parodical allusions to eighteenth-century plays often seem to us obscure enough, but insofar as they are specific rather than generalized we can, with the aid of generations of editors, turn to the printed texts of the passages to which reference is made.

The Knight of the Burning Pestle is, in my opinion, the only stage burlesque in English better than *The Critic*: concerned with more fundamental issues of dramatic theory, more informative about the history of the stage, and more entertaining. Yet it was not Beaumont's play but the Duke of Buckingham's *The Rehearsal*, first produced in 1671 and revived with alterations to bring its satirical targets up to date, that provided Sheridan and his predecessors with their most influential formal model. Garrick alone played the role of Bayes in *The Rehearsal* almost fifty times.[10] The continuing presence of *The Rehearsal* in repertory had much to do with the frequency with which new stage burlesques appeared. It is not the least of Sheridan's accomplishments that *The Critic* largely displaced *The Rehearsal* in repertory.[11] I find unconvincing Simon Trussler's argument that *The Critic's* greater popularity and longevity in performance over other eighteenth-century stage burlesques is attributable to 'its invariable inclusion in complete editions of Sheridan's works . . .'.[12] Mr. Trussler may be justified in arguing that the continuing popularity of Sheridan's burlesque, and the neglect of others written in the eighteenth century with the qualified exception of Fielding's *Tom Thumb*, cannot be attributed to Sheridan's preference for generalized parody of dramatic clichés of language and situation in contrast with the more usual specific parody of earlier plays. As Trussler observes, we may relish the humor of Fielding's *Tom*

Thumb—the lasting popularity of which is only surpassed by *The Critic* among eighteenth-century farces—without identifying the passages Fielding pariodies.[13] Indeed, we could scarcely identify the passages at all without the aid of the 'Annotations of H. Scriblerus Secundus' that Fielding provided when he revised his farce and gave it a new title, *The Tragedy of Tragedies*.

Fielding may well have surpassed Sheridan in the ingenuity of his burlesque of metaphorical extravagances in dialogue. I would find it difficult to choose a passage from the mock blank verse of *The Critic* to place alongside the best-known lines of *The Tragedy of Tragedies* (II.v):

> But Love no Meanness scorns, no Grandeur fears,
> Love often Lords into the Cellar bears,
> And bids the sturdy Porter come up Stairs.
> For what's too high for Love, or what's too low?
> Oh Huncamunca, Huncamunca, oh!

Fielding's unremitting exposition of his mock-heroic fable and his satirical imitations of passages from earlier plays result in a vein of farce that is all his own. If *The Tragedy of Tragedies* mocks dramatic pomposities in a critical spirit not unlike that which animates *The Rehearsal* and *The Critic*, it dispenses with a framing action and conveys its critique of tragic drama by means of parody alone and without the benefit of explanatory comments by 'spectators'. It would be futile to attempt a qualitative comparison of Fielding's and Sheridan's mock verse. But in *The Critic* there is much more than parodic dialogue and situation, and I think the cumulative force of the different methods of burlesque Sheridan employs accounts for the historical fact that *The Critic* has been and still is acted far more frequently than *The Tragedy of Tragedies*—or the other burlesques written by Fielding himself and other dramatists of the century. Editors, publishers, and managers of theatres have been too diligent for 'mute inglorious' masters of the form to lie undisturbed. Several eighteenth-century burlesques other than those written by Fielding and Sheridan merit performance, by university if not by professional groups, but I do not think that any of them, by Fielding or anyone else, will or should rival *The Critic* in popularity.

Burlesques of the stage, and usually of other subjects as well, appeared frequently in the eighteenth-century theatres prior to 1779.[14] Yet few if any of them approximate as closely the form of *The Rehearsal* as *The*

Critic. None of them resembles so closely as *The Critic*—in its first act—the railing comedy of manners of which Wycherley's *Plain Dealer* is the classic example. Gay's *The What d'ye Call It: A Tragi-Comi-Pastoral* of 1715 is, as one would guess from the echo of Polonius's anatomy of drama (*Hamlet*, II.ii), a parody of plays that do not conform to the traditional dramatic genres. Constructed as a play within a play, it resembles *The Knight of the Burning Pestle* more closely than *The Rehearsal*. The simple country folk who are the spectators and actors of *The What d'ye Call It* are much like the rustics of Gay's pastoral poems, *The Shepherd's Week*. Gay, Pope, and Arbuthnot's farce of 1717, *Three Hours After Marriage*, takes as important subjects of ridicule dramatists, drama critics, and theatres; and it includes, if not a 'rehearsal', a short dramatic reading (II). Yet theatrical affairs are subordinated to other satirical preoccupations; and despite the lustre of the authors' names, the prose dialogue is disappointing in quality.[15] Even Gay's masterpiece, *The Beggar's Opera* (1728), is a stage burlesque, with the conventional framing action and interplay between 'spectators' and 'actors'—though its difference from the other burlesques, deriving from its music and its satirical preoccupation with Italian opera, is sufficiently pronounced for it to have little relevance to the tradition leading to *The Critic*.

As I have said in an earlier chapter, Garrick wrote a stage burlesque, *A Peep Behind the Curtain*, in which the actors 'rehearse' not a play but a burletta. Although Garrick's burlesque includes nothing that in form anticipates Sheridan's first act, it puts us in mind of *The Critic* by the conversational interruptions of the rehearsal, with comments on persons and problems encountered in managing the theatre.

Sheridan no doubt took suggestions from Garrick, Buckingham, and other dramatists when he settled to write *The Critic*. He seems also to have taken suggestions, and perhaps some phrases, from an earlier work of his own and the friend of his youth, Nathaniel Halhed. The little that is known about Sheridan's part in the collaboration suggests that it amounted largely to his revision of a burletta on the Amphitryon fable written by Halhed, first called *Juppiter* and later *Ixion*. It is worth remarking that this abortive effort came only two or three years after Garrick's *A Peep Behind the Curtain*, a burletta that was still in repertory. Halhed's text survives in manuscript; Sheridan's revision of it, which significantly for *The Critic* includes a 'rehearsal' scene, survives only in the fragment of it printed by Thomas Moore.[16] A product of Sheridan's dramatic apprenticeship, it was an unsuccessful experiment in the form he brought to perfection in *The Critic*. It reveals him in his youth knowledgeable about what was popular on the London stage of the 1760s. Two seasons before *A Peep Behind the Curtain*, Kane O'Hara had achieved in *Midas: An English Burletta* an even greater popular success than Garrick was to have. *Midas* (which has a complicated history of stage production and authorial revision) was acted twenty-seven times in London during the season of 1765–6.[17] It is easy to understand why Halhed, and through him Sheridan, should have been attracted by the possibilities of burlettas. We may guess that one reason Sheridan could later write *The Critic* with such speed and skill is to be traced to a long maturing of thoughts about dramatic parodies that had a beginning in his collaboration with Halhed.

Like *The Rehearsal* before it, *The Critic* underwent changes with the passing seasons as it was acted in the theatre that brought the topical allusions up to date.[18] Even the first edition of the play, published two years after the first performance, reveals differences from the first acted version as that is represented by the manuscript in the Larpent Collection[19] which was submitted to the Stage Licenser. We may assume that Sheridan himself made the changes which appear in the first edition, 1781; we may not assume that he made the subsequent changes. The later variants in topical allusions are recorded in newspaper reviews and references to the play in letters, as well as in printed editions. In the preface to an edition of 1814, Thomas Dibdin described what seems to have been the practice from the first run of the play: 'The supposed extracts from newspapers, names of, and compliments to particular performers, with other temporary or local passages occurring in this excellent afterpiece, have been always varied to suit the times and circumstances of current representation'.[20] The play had a life of its own in the theatre, at least partially independent of its life in the study.

In 1779 the allusions to living persons, the unmistakable ones (to Sheridan himself and to 'Mr. Louterbourg', among others) and even more perhaps the disguised ones, enhanced the fun. Sheridan followed with restraint a dramatic stratagem that Foote had long used. Of the caricatures in *The Critic*, that of Cumberland as Sir Fretful Plagiary alone merits more than passing comment. Others, such as that of Thomas Vaughn as Mr. Dangle and that of the auctioneer Robert Langford as Mr. Puff, are insufficiently individualized to be consequential, if indeed the identifications can be firmly made.[21]

Sir Fretful Plagiary, like Mrs. Malaprop in *The Rivals*, is a classic exemplar of a perennial foible. If there is no reason to question the traditional and well-documented assumption that Sir Fretful was intended to be and was recognized as a caricature of Richard Cumberland,[22] it should be added that the vain and oversensitive dramatist is much more than that. As early as 4 November 1779, a writer for *The Morning Chronicle* noted that the character bore some resemblance to Sheridan himself.[23] That this is true we may assume from Sheridan's known sensitivity to criticism and his continuing preoccupation in his plays with neurotic sensitivity as a trait of personality. Sir Fretful, like all men, is vulnerable where his passions are engaged—with him, in pride of authorship. Yet in his brooding anxieties and excessive sensitivity to suggestion, he resembles Faulkland of *The Rivals* and Ferdinand of *The Duenna*, even though their anxieties are those of young lovers. The presence in the three plays of a character with the same fault of personality, evident despite differences that are corollaries of their ages, can scarcely be without biographical implications. Sheridan, like his older contemporary James Boswell, wrote repeatedly about a neurotic symptom that interested him because he suffered from it. In Sir Fretful, more than in the two earlier characters (both of whom can plausibly be associated with his courtship of Elizabeth), he turned the insights derived from his personal and self-inflicted sufferings to splendid advantage, creating a character who provides, now as in the eighteenth century, a caution against the inflation of ego to which writers are notoriously prone.

The generalized application of the satire inherent in the portrait of Sir Fretful and the autobiographical strain in it notwithstanding, Sheridan directed the sting conveyed by the character against Cumberland. Yet it is notable that Sir Fretful, the most entertaining but also the cruellest of the caricatures in the play, disappears after the first act. I think it a plausible guess that the reason Sheridan assigned authorship of 'The Spanish Armada' to Mr. Puff rather than to Sir Fretful was a desire to avoid excessive emphasis on the resemblance between the latter and Cumberland. Sir Fretful would seem to have been the obvious choice, as James Boaden explained in the early nineteenth century:

> The pertinacity of Sir Fretful, and his resentment at the liberties taken with his muse, would have been infinitely more relished, than such feelings could be in Puff; who besides has shewn

himself so shrewd an observer of life, and given so masterly a detail of his own efforts, that HE cannot be supposed capable of the childish burlesque, which is to pass upon us as a tragedy written with a serious intention.[24]

Boaden's remarks have force; it is arguable that *The Critic* would be a better play if Sir Fretful had Puff's role as author of the tragedy rehearsed. But this is to leave out of account the response of Sheridan's first audiences, who recognized Sir Fretful as Cumberland.

The resemblances of 'The Spanish Armada', had Sir Fretful been its author, to Cumberland's *The Battle of Hastings* produced at Drury Lane the year before *The Critic* would have been emphasized to the point at which burlesque becomes painful. How closely Mr. Puff's tragedy, in its love intrigue and in its concluding shift of focus to the historical event which provides the title, resembles Cumberland's tragedy can be suggested by the comments of a writer for the *Scot's Magazine*, February 1778:

> Why Mr. Cumberland has chosen to call this play *The battle of Hastings*, we do not see. To be sure we hear something of such a battle in the last act, but almost the whole of the tragedy consists of love-scenes between a disguised prince, and a couple of fond maidens.[25]

We could similarly ask why Mr. Puff has chosen to call his play 'The Spanish Armada'—and to include in it a surfeit of tender love scenes. Sheridan wrote in a tradition deriving from *The Rehearsal*. But in *The Critic* as in all his other plays he stopped short of the acerbity of Restoration drama.

Sheridan's apparent intention to avoid a blunt attack on Cumberland was thwarted by the actor who had the role of Sir Fretful, William Parsons.[26] He dressed like Cumberland, and apparently he imitated Cumberland's mannerisms and facial expressions.[27] James Boaden's account of Parson's interpretation of the role suggests the cruelty that farcical comedy could convey:

> When he [Sir Fretful] stood under the castigation of Sneer, affecting to enjoy criticisms, which made him writhe in agony; when the tears were in his eyes, and he suddenly checked his unnatural laugh, to enable him to stare aghast upon his tormentors; a picture was exhibited of mental anguish and frantic rage,

of mortified vanity and affected contempt, which would almost
deter an author from the pen, unless he could be sure of his firmness under every possible provocation.[28]

Sheridan's text permits such an interpretation without requiring it.
Boaden's description of Parsons as Sir Fretful reminds us of the distance
between a play, and especially a farce, as experienced in print and on the
stage.

Like *The Critic* the earlier stage burlesques are topical in references to
theatrical institutions, and personal in satirical treatment of individuals.
From Buckingham to Sheridan the dramatists employed allusions
their audiences would understand as a principal comic resource. The
topical allusions were inevitably short-lived, rapidly becoming un-
intelligible. Hence in the burlesques that long held the stage, notably
The Rehearsal and *The Critic*, successive revisions were needed to
maintain intelligibility. Yet in the theory of drama conveyed ironically
in the burlesques, there is remarkable continuity and constancy during
the 108 years separating *The Rehearsal* and *The Critic*. With the aid of
the comments of Bayes, author of 'The Two Kings of Brentford', and
the comments and questions of his friends Johnson and Smith as they
watch the actors rehearse, we have little difficulty in understanding
Buckingham's bill of complaints against the form of serious drama
most popular at the time he wrote. We have even less difficulty in
understanding the bill of complaints conveyed in the second and third
acts of *The Critic*. It would not be profitable to examine the implied
theory of drama in the many burlesques written and produced between
1671 and 1779. Yet it is worth noting that, though there is variation in
their principal concerns, they bear a strong family resemblance to
their common progenitor, *The Rehearsal*. Even the best and most
successful of the burlesques written in this interval of time, Fielding's
The Tragedy of Tragedies, reveals similar theoretical preoccupations
although it does not include a mock rehearsal. The constancy in the
theory of drama expressed in the burlesques lends support to the case for
'the survival of neoclassicism'.

As I have said, *The Critic* differs from *The Rehearsal* and other plays
in the tradition most sharply in its first act, which within the conventions of comedy of manners is a critique of theatrical and operatic
affairs. This act, preliminary to the 'rehearsal', enlarges the scope of

Sheridan's dramatic criticism, enabling him to comment on comedy. Buckingham and Fielding, like Sheridan in his two later acts, take the more vulnerable target of the pompositiés of the serious play. *The Rehearsal* includes a few hits at comedy, but they are casual and incidental in relationship to the sustained assault on the rhymed heroic play, which if not precisely tragedy is close enough to it for Buckingham's parody to have generalized relevance to the ethos of many Restoration and eighteenth-century plays that were described as tragedies.

John Gay's *The What d'ye Call It* provides perhaps the nearest approach to Sheridan's central concern in act one, the confounding of dramatic genres. 'And is the Play . . . both a Tragedy and a Comedy?' asks Sir Roger the squire who is providing an entertainment for his neighbours, 'I would have it a Pastoral too: and if you could make it a Farce, so much the better——and what if you crown'd all with a Spice of your Opera?' Sheridan provides all this in *The Critic*, as well as comment on the art of writing plays. But in his first act he includes little that is directed at the satirical targets of *The Rehearsal* except for remarks on plagiarism. Sheridan and Buckingham are alike in the intensity of their preoccupation with plagiarism—though Sheridan unlike his predecessor had, in the malicious charges that had been directed at him, a personal reason for giving attention to the subject. Mr. Bayes describes his 'Rule of Transversion' (I.i); Sneer explains that one of his plays is 'not a translation—only *taken from the French*' (I.i). Writers of the century and more separating *The Rehearsal* and *The Critic* were less permissive about the propriety of an author's borrowing from or reworking an earlier work than we, remembering Pope's *Essay on Criticism*, are likely to assume.[29]

Sheridan's friend the Honorable Richard Fitzpatrick wrote the prologue to *The Critic*, comparing in it Restoration drama with Georgian drama. In Buckingham's time, the prologue goes,

> The tragick Queen, to please a tasteless crowd,
> Had learn'd to bellow, rant, and roar so loud,

that 'frighten'd Nature' deserted her. But by Sheridan's time, the prologue continues,

> The reformation to extremes has run.
> The frantick hero's wild delirium past,
> Now insipidity succeeds bombast. . . .

This prologue (which also includes a comparison between the sexual freedom of Restoration comedy and the prudishness of Georgian comedy) provides a succinct and just though enormously simplified comment on dramatic history. The contrast established between Restoration and Georgian tragedy is as accurate as the brevity of the account of the complicated subject would permit.

Fundamental to the alleged faults in the tragedy of both eras is a departure from what is implied by the metaphorical word 'Nature', a notoriously ambiguous word which can yet, as in Fitzpatrick's prologue, be elucidated by its context. What Bayes says to his two friends (II.i), 'I despise your *Johnson* [sic], and *Beaumont*, that borrow'd all they writt from Nature: I am for fetching it purely out of my own fancy. . .', could appropriately be said by Puff.

Both of them would have been defending the hyperbolical depiction of emotion in the speech of their characters, the clumsiness and ambiguity in the exposition of their characters' motives, and the violations of probability and even possibility in the events which make up their plots. Both Bayes and Puff depict extravagant and unconvincing codes of heroic conduct and the emotional anguish that results when the codes conflict with sexual but idealized love.

The rhetorical extravagancies to which Bayes and Puff rise merit parallel illustration. Cloris speaks in *The Rehearsal* (II.iii):

> As some tall Pine, which we, on *Aetna*, find
> T'have stood the rage of many a boyst'rous wind,
> Feeling without, that flames within do play,
> Which would consume his Root and Sap away;
> He spreads his worsted Arms unto the skies,
> Silently grieves, all pale, repines and dies. . . .

Tilburina speaks in *The Critic* (II.ii):

> 'Now has the whispering breath of gentle morn,
> Bad Nature's voice, and Nature's beauty rise;
> While orient Phoebus with unborrow'd hues,
> Cloaths the wak'd loveliness which all night slept
> In heav'nly drapery!'

Sheridan parodies the 'insipidity' (to use Fitzpatrick's word in the prologue) of clichés of dialogue; Buckingham parodies the hyperbolical 'rant' of a specific passage, in Dryden's *The Conquest of Granada*

(Part One, V.iii). Although the dramatists employ different satirical methods, the two passages illustrate alike the loss of the illusion of truth—or conformity with 'Nature'—needed if tragedy is to elicit the desired response. Failing to succeed by traditional means, both Bayes and Puff took refuge in ornate language and in the nonverbal appeal of ceremonial and of elaborate painted scenery.

How did Sheridan, in his own time, achieve supremacy in farce as well as in comedy of manners and comic opera? There are several plausible explanations. His superb prose style, evident in the precision of diction in his dialogue, enabled him to convey rapidly ludicrous confusions of priorities in human values. The satirical strategy is not unlike that in Pope's *Rape of the Lock*. As Mr. Dangle reads the newspapers in the opening scene, he turns impatiently from reports about the danger of a foreign invasion to the columns devoted to the theatres. More than Sheridan's prose style and sensitivity to incongruity are apparent. In his caricature of Mr. Dangle, a man obsessed with theatrical affairs, as in his other caricatures of persons in the grip of idiosyncracies, Sheridan reverts with greater emphasis to the mode of burlesque he had used consistently since *The Rivals*. Like all caricatures, whether in the graphic arts or in language, Sheridan's depend for their impact on a choice of subjects that seem relevant to the experience of audiences and an emphasis on qualities that are ludicrous and are also convincing as typical of the subjects.

In the first act of *The Critic*, and less obviously in the second and third, Sheridan reconciles the mode of burlesque with the conventions of comedy of manners. The resemblances between the hypocritical conversational malice of the first act to the conversational habits of Lady Sneerwell's circle do not require elucidation. The first act of *The Critic* provides more than a framing action for the rehearsal which follows. It introduces sharply realized characters—or caricatures— whose presence animates the succeeding acts. Sir Fretful disappears, having suffered enough, but Dangle, Puff, and Sneer remain to talk about Puff's play—and to reveal more of the personal qualities epitomized in their names. The prolongation of interplay among the characters of the framing action, as in *The Knight of the Burning Pestle*, provides a defence against the tedium which is a hazard of even the cleverest mockery of bad drama.

In *The Rehearsal*, the author of 'The Two Kings of Brentford',

I

Bayes, and his friends Smith and Johnson appear throughout the play and carry on a conversation about what they see on stage. But Smith and Johnson are as little particularized as their names are unusual. They represent the common sense of general humanity, and their remarks, a very large number of them in the form of questions, serve as often to elicit explanations from Bayes as to comment on his play. Of the three attending the rehearsal, only Bayes emerges as a character with personal and idiosyncratic qualities. He is above all, like most of his literary descendants including Puff, an unself-critical and vain dramatist who cannot perceive the bombast and implausibility in the plays he writes. Yet if the archetypal author of pompous dramatic absurdity, Bayes is also a caricature of Dryden, who after D'Avenant's death in 1668 had figuratively worn bay leaves as Poet Laureate. While doing so he continued to write rhymed heroic plays that, although popular in the theatres, were vulnerable then as now to unsympathetic critics. Buckingham[30] was as ready as Sheridan a century later to identify a satirical target; and Buckingham, under no such constraints as Georgian England imposed on dramatists, could make sport of Dryden's private life—as in a reference (I) to Dryden's alleged liaison with the actress Anne Reeves. Yet despite the personal references and the numerous hits at *The Conquest of Granada* and other plays by Dryden (as well as by other men), it is open to question whether the portrait of Dryden as Bayes strikes harder than the portrait of Cumberland as Sir Fretful. A more able satirist than Buckingham, Sheridan had no need of reference to Cumberland's private life to score his points.

Sheridan provides a wide range of satirical reference, giving attention to social and particularly political subjects as well as dramatic ones. With only mild overstatement we can say that talk about 'The Spanish Armada' in the second and third acts serves as a continuation of the specialized form of comedy of manners that makes up the first act. In this aspect of his play, Sheridan departs from eighteenth-century as well as Restoration precedent.

The Critic had an advantage over the earlier burlesques in the magnificence and skill exhibited in its mounting. 'With regard to the . . . stage decorations,' wrote the reviewer for *The Morning Chronicle*, 1 November 1779, with a trace of irony, 'when our readers recollect, that the piece was written by the manager, they need not be told that neither pains nor cost were spared to give it every recommendation in the power of the Theatre.' *The Morning Post*, 1 November 1779, describes in detail what the first audiences saw on stage, conveying something of the ceremonial and visual aspect of *The Critic*, for which the famous painter Philippe Jacques De Loutherbourg was responsible:

> The piece was decorated likewise with three beautiful scenes, designed and executed under the immediate direction of Mr. De Loutherbourgh; viz. a view of the Thames, and Gravesend from Tilbury Fort,—the Governor's tent in a grove, —and a sea view, with a representation of an action between the British fleet and the Spanish Armada, wherein after great part of the latter are destroyed by fireships, the former appear triumphantly pursuing them to martial music, playing 'Britannia rule the Waves!'—After this, a mock procession takes place of the several rivers of this island, who walk with their various symbols in their hands, old father *Thames* bringing up the rear in his crystal car; this, with a dance of river *nymphs* and *godlings*, closed the piece. . . .

De Loutherbourg was employed by Sheridan at Drury Lane from 1777 to 1782.[31] Known to historians of art for his romantic landscapes in a style that anticipates Turner's, he had come to England from the Continent in 1771, having already earned a reputation with his paintings. Garrick had employed him at Drury Lane as Sheridan did a few years later. He was an innovative technician in scene design as well as an accomplished artist. Sybil Rosenfeld has described some innovations of his that suggest the technical resources known to and made use of by Sheridan in planning the pageant that closes *The Critic* as well as the spectacles that appear earlier in the play. Miss Rosenfeld mentions De Loutherbourg's 'use of small models or cutouts which passed across the stage and were moved mechanically. In *Alfred*, 1773, his first production, complete models of ships by the marine painter, Serres, took part in a naval review. Even more ambitious in *Queen Mab*, 1775, in a scene of a Thames regatta, barges were rowed to music, each oar keeping a regular stroke.' The pageant with which *The Critic* ends provided full scope for the skills of De Loutherbourg, who had devised, among other things, 'Wave machines turning on spindles'[32] that could add verisimilitude to the representation of the English victory over the Spanish fleet.

The Critic was first performed in October 1779. Sheridan was first elected to the House of Commons in September 1780. The two events are not causally related, but neither are they totally unrelated. Sheridan, already associated politically with Charles James Fox, was elected as a candidate in opposition to Lord North's Ministry. Mr. Puff's 'Spanish Armada' includes a subtle burlesque of Lord North and the inept attempt of his Ministry, during the months before *The Critic* appeared, to prepare the nation and its navy to repel a threatened invasion by a combined French and Spanish fleet.

Following the military disaster suffered when in October 1777 General Burgoyne (whom Sheridan invited in 1779 to a reading of *The Critic*) surrendered his army at Saratoga, the French could perceive the trend of events in the American War. With their losses during the Seven Years War fresh in mind, they formed an alliance with the Americans which in 1778 led to war between France and Britain. In the following year Spain joined France against Britain. By summer of that year, 1779, the British feared, with good cause, an invasion supported by the combined French and Spanish fleets. That it did not come was owing to the mistakes and misfortunes of their enemies rather than to their own decisiveness and energy. In any event, by late October, when Drury Lane first presented *The Critic*, the enemy fleet had retired and the danger of invasion had passed.

The events of the summer and autumn of 1779 probably had much more to do with the selection of the subject of Puff's play than Cumberland's *Battle of Hastings*.[33] King George himself referred to the defeat of the Spanish Armada in an effort to rouse his subjects to the needed effort to defend his Kingdom. 'It was the vigour of mind shown by Queen Elizabeth and her subjects,' he wrote in June 1779, 'added to the assistance of Divine Providence, that saved this island when attacked by the Spaniards.'[34] Yet the King kept in office a chief Minister who, at that time at least, lacked 'vigour of mind'.

Sheridan had to be circumspect in his disguised allusions to the chief Minister and his conduct in office. During the fifty years since Gay's *The Beggar's Opera*, the position of Stage Licenser had been established. Furthermore, dramatists and their audiences had by habit become less audacious. Yet Sheridan's choice of the defeat of the Spanish Aramada as the nominal subject of the play in rehearsal, and his depiction of Queen Elizabeth's chief Minister Lord Burleigh as so preoccupied with his own thoughts that he does not speak, had political meaning in the autumn of 1779.

In comparison with Gay's insistent and varied references in *The Beggar's Opera* to Sir Robert Walpole, Sheridan's allusion to Lord North himself is brief and oblique, so much so that it is now easily overlooked. Yet it was noted during the play's first run. *The Morning Post*, 1 November 1779, includes a remark that would have been understood by those in the audience who read the newspapers: '. . . Puff's interpretation of that Prime Minister's *thoughts*', the journalist wrote, referring to Lord Burleigh '[was not] by any means an ill-timed stroke of political satire.'

Burleigh's brief role in 'The Spanish Armada' (III.i) is a totally mute one. In answer to a question from Dangle about Burleigh's silence after he enters and *'goes slowly to a chair and sits'*, Puff replies:

> Egad, I thought you'd ask me that—yes it is a very likely thing —that a Minister in his situation, with the whole affairs of the nation on his head, should have time to talk!—but hush! or you'll put him out.

When Sneer exclaims that he can scarcely be put out if he is not to say anything, Puff answers that Burleigh's part is to *'think'*. A moment later the character *'comes forward, shakes his head and exit'*. Puff explains the meaning of the gesture:

> Why, by that shake of the head, he gave you to understand that even tho' they had more justice in their cause and wisdom in their measures—yet, if there was not a greater spirit shown on the part of the people—the country would at last fall a sacrifice to the hostile ambition of the Spanish monarchy.[35]

It would be difficult to find in any other play acted at Drury Lane or Covent Garden during the twelve years of North's Ministry more direct criticism of him.

At the time of the crisis in British affairs during the months prior to the première of *The Critic*, Lord North suffered from what we would be inclined to call a 'depression'. He had long felt himself inadequate to his responsibilities and had remained in office only in obedience to the King. Added to the reverses in America, unrest in Ireland, and the danger of a military invasion of England itself, North experienced personal sorrow as well. Less than a week after the Spanish ambassador delivered, on 16 June 1779, what was in effect a declaration of war, one of North's sons died. North continued to perform his duties, but neither thereafter nor before with anything approximating the vigor and decision the national crisis required.[36] The near-paralysis of the leadership of government was accompanied by ineptitude or inaction by many in subordinate positions including naval officers such as Sir Charles Hardy, whom Dangle mentions in the opening speech of *The Critic*. Lord North's Parliamentary opponents, including Charles James Fox, did not allow the inadequacies of the Ministry to go unnoticed. Sheridan's cautious caricature of Lord North in the guise of Lord Burleigh provides in epitome the thrust of the Opposition's charge that the government lacked a leadership with initiative and skill.

Sheridan's commentary on the inadequacy of the nation's defences is not confined to his depiction of Lord Burleigh. The subject of the play in rehearsal carried its own ironic commentary. By calling up the memory of that famous victory, long a point of focus for national pride, Sheridan could convey a damaging comparison with the current condition of Britain. His literary strategy is not unlike Pope's in his imitation of Horace's epistle *To Augustus*: use of an overtly laudatory comparison of George III and his kingdom to a sovereign and his empire in Antiquity to convey a harsh judgment. Sheridan, like Pope before him, moves from generalized criticism to specifics—as in Puff's scene (III.i) depicting the quality of recruits for the army raised by justices of the peace:

Justice.
'Are all the volunteers without?
Constable.

'They are.
Some ten in fetters, and some twenty drunk.
Justice.
'Attends the youth, whose most opprobrious fame
And clear convicted crimes have stampt him soldier?

The constable assures the justice that the youth is present,

'. . . eager to repay
The blest reprieve that sends him to the fields
Of glory. . . .

The justice's confident hope that the youth will now defend his country's laws

With half the spirit he has broke them all!'

would have generated laughter in an audience of 1779, but scarcely conviction that Lord North's Ministry could organize an adequate defence of the nation. Sheridan's audience would have associated the incompetence depicted in Puff's 'Spanish Armada' with 1779 rather than 1588.

After the burlesque rehearsal, applicable at once to national affairs and to earlier drama, comes Sheridan's concluding call to arms, conveyed in spectacle and music:

> . . . *Scene changes to the sea—the fleets engage—the musick plays 'Britons strike home.'—Spanish fleet destroyed by fire-ships, &c. English fleet advances—musick plays 'Rule Britannia.'*

And finally, to an accompaniment of music by Handel, the play closes with a symbolic procession of the English rivers, which are identified by their emblems.[37]

Sheridan follows the familiar tradition of loyalty to the Crown by the Opposition to the King's Ministry. There is no mistaking the emotions aroused by a rendering of 'Rule Britannia'. For the first three-quarters of the eighteenth century, Britons had indeed ruled the waves.[38] Yet in 1779 they found themselves, after the alliance of France and Spain, confronted with approximately equal naval power. It was a novel and alarming development, the more dangerous because of the inadequacies of their government. In the pageant which closes *The Critic*, Sheridan could contrast the Navy in 1779 and the Navy in earlier times, even while exhorting his countrymen to patriotic zeal.

After his election to Parliament the following year, he could carry on his criticism of the Ministry in speeches from the floor of the House of Commons.

6

Whig Oratory on Stage, *Pizarro*

Pizarro remains an enigma in Sheridan's career. How could the author of *The Critic* publicly associate himself with a play that—in print if not on the stage—resembled Mr. Puff's 'Spanish Armada'? How could a man who twenty years earlier had revealed an acute sensitivity to emotional pretentiousness indulge the extravagant heroics of *Pizarro*? He was not in the first instance responsible for the play, which is and was acknowledged to be an adaptation from the German of Kotzebue, *Die Spanier in Peru*, but it is a free adaptation in which more than language is original. Sheridan had an important share of responsibility for it, and he was proud of it and its enormous success in the theatre. To be sure, it is an operatic tragedy which was splendidly mounted in the new Drury Lane Theatre, and a reading of it cannot convey the impression made on the early audiences. Yet Sheridan promptly published *Pizarro*.

Despite the traditional disparagement of *Pizarro* by students of the drama, it is not without its claim on our attention. It provides a major link between Sheridan's dramatic and his Parliamentary careers. It is his only play written after his election to the House of Commons in 1780, just as it is the only one of his plays including emphatic political comment. Even in the eighteenth century, remarkable for the political prominence of literary men, Sheridan is unique among the major literary figures in the political prominence and influence he achieved. Addison as Secretary of State held higher office, but it is hard to think of Addison's brief tenure of that position or of his previous career in Whig politics as providing any real parallel to Sheridan's thirty years in

Parliament, many of them spent as a principal leader of the Opposition to Pitt and as a principal adviser of the Prince of Wales. Addison was a silent member of the House of Commons; Sheridan one of the most eloquent orators in the history of Parliament. He is the single man of high accomplishment who achieved comparable success as a writer and a politician. Swift, Steele, and even Addison were primarily writers whose pens won for them political influence or office. Sheridan too found his way into politics by his early literary successes. But his triumphs in Parliament and in Court intrigue soon equalled—if to contemporaries they did not eclipse—his early triumphs in the theatre. It was not an unqualified advantage to him in Parliament to be known as a man of the theatre. Pitt himself made a sarcastic reference, in a debate in the House of Commons, to his plays—only to be answered in one of the cleverest of all the retorts of this famous wit: if he should ever again turn to the drama, he replied to the very young Chancellor of the Exchequer, he should be tempted to the presumption of trying to improve the character of the 'Angry Boy' in Jonson's *Alchemist*.[1] The fact that Sheridan could be chided for achievements unequalled in Georgian drama is a measure of the political and social eminence he had reached.

Pizarro came late in his career, and it is disappointing. Yet the play is not to be explained as the result of a premature senility. Even assuming that he was aged by dissipation and the vicissitudes of his life, he had not, at forty-seven, outlived his powers. He was and would remain for another decade a leading political figure. If in the twenty years since *The Critic* his writing for the theatre had been confined to short entertainments and to revisions of the work of other people, he had won world fame by his Parliamentary oratory, which in that age of Burke, Fox, and Pitt required the utmost capacity in skills akin to those required in literary composition. A man who could hold his own in debate with Pitt was in full possession of his faculties.

It is not in a decline of his powers but in an alteration of his style, his interests, and his objectives that the explanation for *Pizarro* is to be sought. Sheridan no longer had the time nor the inclination for such extended literary work as he had expended on *The School for Scandal*. He had become a political personage, no doubt in his own mind and in those of his associates a more desirable condition than that of a leading dramatist, and in *Pizarro* he wrote like one: in the ideas to which he gave dramatic form as well as in his mode of expression. He did not write an allegorical play except in the generalized sense that the title character represents Napoleon Bonaparte.[2] Yet, as I shall argue, he wrote a Whig play—a play that celebrates the social and political philosophy of the Opposition to Pitt, even though it includes a pledge of loyalty to the King and of opposition to the French. The pledge of loyalty won the play some bi-partisan support.[3] But certain of Pitt's propagandists saw clearly enough, and explained in detail, the Whiggish implications of the play. In that time of danger of invasion, Sheridan supported the government in defensive measures against the French, just as he had two years earlier during the Navy mutinies, but he remained a principal member of the Opposition to Pitt's Ministry— and as Pitt himself said, Sheridan drew in *Pizarro* from his own speeches.

This is not to say that Sheridan's motive in writing *Pizarro* was exclusively or even primarily political. He could after all make himself heard in the House of Commons. No doubt his principal motive was financial: his awareness that with a modicum of effort he could refurbish Kotzebue's play and meet the current taste for German drama. His chronic indebtedness is notorious, and at that time Drury Lane, which provided his principal source of income, was in more than the customary financial straits.[4] Sheridan had not lost his shrewd capacity to evaluate current theatrical fashions, and he would have remembered the success of Benjamin Thompson's adaptation from Kotzebue, *The Stranger*, the year before. Reasons enough for the proprietor of Drury Lane to choose a play by Kotzebue—not in German, which he could not read, but in translation[5]— as the basis for his work.

Yet his choice of the particular play, *Die Spanier in Peru*, must have turned on its appropriateness as a framework for the exposition of political attitudes and opinions he had long expressed in Parliament. It is scarcely coincidence that Davenant, Dryden, and Voltaire had long before used the Spanish treatment of the Indians as the subject of plays which condemn European exploitation of a subjugated people, a favourite subject with Sheridan since the trial of Warren Hastings. Davenant in *The Cruelty of the Spaniards in Peru* (1658), Dryden in *The Indian Emperour* (1665), and Voltaire in *Alzire ou les Américains* (1736) had included scenes depicting Spanish atrocity in the New World. All three plays are coloured by the humanitarian protests of Bartolomé de las Casas, who appears as a dramatic character in *Pizarro*. There is no reason to assume that Sheridan knew these earlier plays. He could quite independently perceive, as other dramatists had before him, that the *conquistadores'* treatment of the Indians provided a classic example of inhumanity to a defenceless people.

In any event, he need not have looked to the plays of Davenant, Dryden, and Voltaire for literary models. He had others closer at hand. 'It is . . . probable that this Play would have a much stronger impression,' wrote a critic in *The True Briton*, 25 May 1799, 'if the story were not so familiar to the Audience. We have already had it in the Opera of *Idalide* and in the Play of *Columbus*.' Just as in his comedies, Sheridan follows dramatic patterns that had been used by other writers—and scene designers and carpenters—of the recent past. *Idalide* and Thomas Morton's *Columbus* derive from the pseudo-historical romance, Jean François Marmontel's *Les Incas, ou la destruction de l'empire du Pérou* (1777), Kotzebue's source for *Die Spanier in Peru* and thus indirectly of *Pizarro*. *Idalide* and *Columbus* had both been performed in London earlier in the same decade as Sheridan's play: the opera at the Pantheon Theatre in 1791 and the play at Covent Garden in 1792. The shared literary ancestry with *Pizarro* accounts for the many shared qualities among the three works.

'*Idalide, o sia La Vergine del Sole*, A Serious Opera,' seems to have been sung in Italian, to judge from the libretto (attributed to Ferdinando Moretti, though not on the title page), which in the London edition of 1791 is printed with the Italian and English texts on facing pages. The names of the singers are Italian; a prefatory 'Argument' in English looks as though it was intended for an audience which could not follow the dialogue in Italian. The opera carries its history lightly. The history in fact serves principally as a framework to support the love intrigue and as justification for the spectacle provided by Incan ceremonial.

Thomas Morton's *Columbus: Or, A World Discovered* reveals even more strongly than *Idalide* a kinship with *Pizarro*, extending in this instance to the presence of two characters, Alonzo and Cora, in both Morton's and Sheridan's plays. Apart from these two characters and their relationship to one another, however, there is little similarity of plot between the plays. Yet in other respects, the plays are much alike: in indifference to historical reality, in florid diction, in the idealization of Indians as uncorrupted primitives, in latent hostility to the Spaniards and to Roman Catholicism, in the exploitation of Indian ritual as exotic background for dramatic action, in extensive use of painted scenes and other stage properties. Morton's stage directions suggest that he attempted to achieve a spectacle similar to that in performances of *Pizarro*. An elaborate description of the stage design and the commencement of the action appears at the beginning of Act I:

> On one side of the stage a flight of steps, with a Portico leading to the Temple of the Sun.—In the background the sea. Time, sun-rise.
> Catalpo *and Priests from the Temple, who range themselves—then enter* Orozimbo—*they bow to him as he passes.*
> Orozimbo, *prostrating himself to the sun.*

Similar stage directions, though less elaborate, appear throughout the play, and collectively they convince the reader that Morton, like Sheridan after him, used spectacle as an emblem of the heroic code of conduct by which the virtuous characters, Indians and Europeans alike, regulate their lives. This play will convince us that *Pizarro* was no isolated phenomenon in the 1790s.

Pizarro was written in haste, such great haste that it was not completed until the final rehearsals, and newspaper reviews reveal that important changes were made after the first performance. The circumstances of Sheridan's career assure us that he could not have made a study of the historical records of the Spanish conquest of Peru. His play follows that of Kotzebue, which in turn follows Marmontel's historical romance, *Les Incas*. This bastard literary ancestry notwithstanding, *Pizarro* includes, in the characterization of Las-Casas, an echo of a famous controversy of sixteenth-century Spain. This Dominican monk had denounced the Spanish exploitation of the Indians so bitterly in his *Brevíssima relación de la destruyción de las Indias* (1552) as to have led to an investigation of his charges by a royal commission. Although the commission rejected Las Casas' charges, his work long inspired critics of Spanish imperial policy. It is not fanciful to think that the existence of such a character in a play by Sheridan owes something to the dramatist's recollection of his role in the trial of Warren Hastings. Sheridan had as strong a claim as anyone except Burke to regard himself as the English champion of the East Indians, and as such in a position not unlike that of Las Casas with respect to the Indians of Spanish America. 'Do not, I implore you,' says Las-Casas to Pizarro and his lieutenants (I), 'renew the foul barbarities which your insatiate avarice has inflicted on this wretched, unoffending race!' The dramatic character's speeches are at once representative of what the sixteenth-century monk had written and reminiscent of what Sheridan had said against Hastings. 'Generously and freely,' Las-Casas reminds the Spanish leaders, 'did they share with you their comforts, their treasures, and their homes: you repaid them by fraud, oppression, and dishonour.' It is small wonder that Pitt commented after a performance of the play that he had heard it all before.[6]

Pitt, Sheridan, and everyone else interested in politics would have been aware that the depiction of Pizarro and the Spaniards in Peru resembled Sheridan's earlier depiction of Hastings and the English in India. Sheridan invited comparison of the play with his speeches by repeating, in Rolla's address to the Peruvian warriors, his widely remembered simile of a vulture and a lamb. 'Like a vulture with her harpy talons grappled in the vitals of the . . . lamb,' Sheridan had said in Westminster Hall, 13 June, 1788, 'they flap away the lesser kites, and then they call it protection! It is the protection of the vulture to the lamb....'[7] 'They offer us their protection—', Rolla says of the Spaniards (II.ii), 'Yes, such protection as vultures give to lambs—covering and devouring them!' Thomas Moore, Sheridan's biographer, justly remarked that 'This speech, to whose popular sentiments the play owed much of its success, was chiefly made up by Sheridan of loans from his own oratory'[8]—his oratory directed against the French, we may add, as well as that directed against Warren Hastings.

Sheridan's glances at English policy, in Rolla's speech and throughout the play, are not confined to the alleged atrocities in India. He writes as a monarchist, of course, and as one who is finally convinced that the danger from the French is real. He also writes as a champion of liberty and human rights. 'I have not warred against my native land,' declares Alonzo (III.iii), the Spanish officer who has deserted Pizarro to join the Peruvians, 'but against those who have usurped its power. The banners of my country, when first I followed arms beneath them, were Justice, Faith, and Mercy.' This is sufficiently generalized to leave an application to English politics in doubt. The more obvious double meaning would apply to recent events in France. Yet Alonzo's declaration of principles, appearing in a play by a man who had long been second only to Fox in the force of his criticism of the government's policies, may not be free of Whig innuendo. Sheridan was writing at the end of a decade that had witnessed suspension of the *Habeas Corpus* Act, limitations imposed on the press, harsh punishment of critics of the government, resistance to Parliamentary reform, and resistance to the abolition of the Slave Trade.[9] He had been a leading participant in the Parliamentary debates, consistently opposing the repressive measures Pitt had undertaken in response to the French Revolution. He and Lord Holland were alone among the important politicians to oppose the Prime Minister's acts of 1799 and 1800 directed against trade unionism. Sheridan and Pitt had entered Parliament in the same year, 1780, and nineteen years later Sheridan might not unreasonably have thought that the Prime Minister had abandoned the humanitarian principles that they had earlier shared.

If *Pizarro* includes a generalized defence of humanitarian principles, it can be interpreted, I think, as having special relevance to the current debates about the slave trade. From the Spaniards' rapacious abuse of the Peruvians to the Europeans' traffic in slaves there is but little distance in inhumanity. When a Peruvian grandfather explains to his incredulous grandson that the Spaniards would drag the boy away from him (II.iv), we may catch an echo of Sheridan's opposition in Parliament to Britain's complicity in the institution of slavery. 'For his part,' he is reported as having said in the House of Commons, 23 April 1790, 'he required no evidence—no further information to convince him, that the power possessed by the West India merchant over the slave was such a power as no man ought to have over another.'[10] His position on the issue was consistent throughout his career. He does not allude to it in *Pizarro*; we have no warrant for regarding the play as propaganda for the suppression of the slave trade. Yet the bare simplicity of *Pizarro*, its resemblance to a moral fable in its clarity of outline and unqualified distinction between evil and good, permits an application to slavery as well as to colonial exploitation. He had himself made something approaching that application in his Hastings speeches. 'We are challenged by all the laws of God and man to relieve millions of our fellow-creatures from a state of misery and oppression,' he had said in the House of Commons, 7 February 1787. 'It is true we do not see the swarms of human beings who call upon us for relief. We do not hear the bitter lamentations of those who are ready to perish.'[11] William Wilberforce, religious leader of the movement against the slave trade, attended and applauded a performance of *Pizarro*, even though for the preceding twenty years he had not attended the theatre.[12] The idealization of humble and primitive people, in the drama as in political oratory, had corollaries, as Tory journalists understood, in political action.

Sheridan's political stance in *Pizarro* has been obscured by the fact
that the most famous speech in the play—Rolla's address to the Peruvian
warriors before battle (II.ii)—is intended as an appeal to the English for
firmness at a time of danger of French invasion. Because Sheridan had
long been one of the most outspoken critics of the English war against
the French, his inclusion of Rolla's speech (which is not in Kotzebue)
can seem incongruous with his role in the Parliamentary Opposition.
The speech is unambiguous in its simple allegorical equation of the
Spanish and Pizarro with the French and Bonaparte: 'THEY follow an
Adventurer whom they fear—and obey a power which they hate—.'
Yet in all essentials the speech is anticipated by what Sheridan had said
in Parliament in 1797 and 1798, years in which for good reason he had
reversed his stand on the French.[13] Referring in the House of Commons,
26 April 1798, to the threat of an invasion led by Bonaparte, he was
scarcely less emphatic in his appeal to his countrymen than he was to be
in the play: 'For confident I am, that, as soon as one drop of English
blood shall be shed by a Frenchman on English ground, the English
valour will that moment rise to a pitch equal to what its most sanguine
friends can expect, or its warmest admirers can desire. . . .'[14] The orator
was almost as florid in his diction as the dramatist, and he was as
fervently opposed to Bonaparte. Yet in neither of his roles had Sheridan
given up his convictions as humanitarian spokesman for oppressed
people.

Even the best orations of politicians make dull reading in later times,
and too much of *Pizarro* sounds like an oration. The dialogue has the
hyperbole and oversimplification of political debate. The characters
speak in abstractions and superlatives. Rolla's contrast between the
Peruvians and the Spanish aggressors, in which he discriminates between
constitutional monarchy and tyrannical absolutism, has the clarity of
wartime propaganda. His analysis of the Spaniards' motives recalls
what Sheridan had said in the House of Commons the year before
about the motives of the French. 'What, then, is their object?' Sheridan
had asked in his speech of 26 April 1798. And he had answered his own
question:

> They come for what they really want: they come for ships, for
> commerce, for credit, and for capital. Yes; they come for the
> sinews, the bones; for the marrow, and for the very heart's
> blood of Great Britain.[15]

All this is implicit in Rolla's contrast between the Peruvians and the Spaniards:

> Your generous spirit has compared as mine has, the motives, which, in a war like this, can animate *their* minds, and OURS.— THEY, by a strange frenzy driven, fight for power, for plunder, and extended rule—WE, for our country, our altars, and our homes.

This is an appeal to the primary emotions which the play consistently indulges: here, of patriotism; at other times of familial love or noble friendship.

Rolla's oratorical style resembles that of many of Sheridan's speeches —but with the important difference that in the best of the speeches the rhetorical flourishes were held in check by the ballast of supporting factual and analytical detail. We are likely to underestimate Sheridan's achievements in oratory because of our modern preference for the understated and closely analytical over the hyperbolical and emotional argument. Unimpassioned plain speaking did not win Sheridan his reputation. Yet he worked up his subjects before speaking, and in his major efforts, such as the Hastings speeches, he showed an extraordinary command of intricate historical exposition. We may recognize the affinity between the dialogue of *Pizarro* and Sheridan's oratory; but we may not in fairness assume that the oratory was consistently like the play. Sheridan spoke in Parliament to an audience which included men of the highest intelligence, who could distinguish between bombast and analysis of issues, and he won his reputation with closely reasoned if impassioned argument which was an accepted stylistic convention of the period.

Rolla's speech to the Pervuian warriors is Sheridan's but most of the play derives from Kotzebue. It is not for that reason the less relevant to English politics. The vogue of German drama in England reached its peak at a time when the military ambitions and capabilities of Bonaparte were becoming steadily more alarming. The Navy mutinies of 1797 had revealed a vulnerability to a French invasion, in which, it was feared, the French might gain support from English dissidents. In retrospect we may conclude that Pitt's government exaggerated the danger from sedition, but we can understand why the government should have been suspicious of literary imports from the Continent, including those from German drama. The adaptations from Kotzebue came under attack from Tory writers, one of them George Canning, the future Foreign Secretary and Prime Minister.

From 20 November 1797 to 9 July 1798, Canning was a principal contributor to *The Anti-Jacobin, or Weekly Examiner*, a journal no less remarkable for its literary distinction than for its ultraconservatism. As hostile to the French Revolution and as unqualifiedly opposed to political innovation as had been Edmund Burke, Canning and his collaborators found targets in literary works that could even remotely be interpreted as immoral, egalitarian, or subversive. Frequently they used burlesque as their satirical medium, as they did in *The Rovers*, a mock German drama published in *The Anti-Jacobin* for 4 June 1798— less than three months after Drury Lane had produced an adaptation from Kotzebue, *The Stranger*, written by Benjamin Thompson with assistance from Sheridan.[16] Lest their readers miss their satirical points, the authors of *The Rovers* emulated Martinus Scriblerus in providing their composition with prefatory comments and explanatory footnotes. ' "Destroy the frame of society,—decompose its parts,—" ' explains 'Our ingenious Correspondent, Mr. HIGGINS,'

> and set the elements fighting one against another,—insulated and individual,—and every man for himself (stripped of prejudice, of bigotry, and of feeling for others) against the remainder of his species;—and there is then some hope of a totally new *order of things*,—of a *Radical Reform* in the present corrupt System of the World.
>
> The German Theatre appears to proceed on this judicious plan. And I have endeavoured to contribute my mite towards extending its effect and its popularity.[17]

The Stranger was one of the principal targets of *The Rovers*. Sheridan had reason to anticipate criticism from the Tories when he wrote *Pizarro* the next year.

After *The Anti-Jacobin, or Weekly Examiner* suspended publication in the summer of 1798, it was followed by a journal of similar title and political bias, *The Anti-Jacobin Review and Magazine*, and again the German drama came under attack. 'It is the evident tendency of this piece,' an anonymous critic wrote in the issue for October 1798 about an adaptation written by Elizabeth Inchbald,

K

as, indeed, of most of the pieces of the modern German school, and of its disciples in this country, to render the upper classes of society, objects of indignation or contempt; and to confine all virtue, and every noble quality, to the lower classes of the community; and, at the same time, to propagate and diffuse the principles of the *new philosophism*.

These remarks are so similar to the criticism of 'Kotzebue's Pizarro'— that is, Sheridan's play—in the issue for June 1799 as to suggest that the same critic was at work. 'One most striking feature distinguishes all of Kotzebue's dramas—the great are *vicious*, the low are *virtuous*. . . . In *Pizarro* we have a chief or general painted in the most infamous characters. . .'. Not Sheridan but the German dramatist is the nominal target of all this (though the title of Sheridan's play is used), but in June 1799 there could have been few literate residents of London who would have failed to make the required equation. 'Let us, for God's sake, look with a little more circumspection,' the reviewer exclaims, 'at the claims of these German philosophers, before we so readily admit the value of them.'[18]

The most comprehensive of the hostile explications of the political doctrine of *Pizarro* came several years later from William Cobbett who, his later career notwithstanding, was at the time committed to the Tory position. In 1804 he devoted a book, *The Political Proteus, a View of the Public Character and Conduct of R. B. Sheridan, Esq.*, to a condemnatory account of Sheridan's career; and in one of the 'letters' which comprise the book he wrote at length about *Pizarro*. Cobbett used the play in support of his accusation that Sheridan was indeed 'protean' in his ability to make unprincipled and opportunistic changes in his political attitudes, as in Sheridan's abandonment of his earlier opposition to the war against France and inclusion of a show of defiance to Bonaparte in the play; but he did not stop with a mere charge of inconsistency. Turning to the most famous passage in the play, Rolla's address to the Peruvian warriors, Cobbett professed to find anti-monarchical sentiments in Sheridan's phrasing. 'The throne WE honour,' says Rolla, 'is the PEOPLE'S CHOICE.' This would seem to us to be unexceptionable political doctrine in the century after Parliament had confirmed the claims of the House of Hanover, but as Cobbett's remarks make clear, the subject remained sensitive. Just the year before *Pizarro* was first performed, George III had removed Fox from the

Privy Council for repeating a toast, 'The People, our Sovereign,' made earlier by the Duke of Norfolk. The alleged implications of Sheridan's phrasing are explained by Cobbett:

> ... what shall we say, when your 'truly English' play-vamping loyalty has enlightened Rolla, so long before the poor fellow's time, with the most brilliant illumination of the republican societies here, affiliated and unaffiliated, of which you yourself [Sheridan] were a member? You use the very phrases of their favourite maxim, that the *throne*, which, by the bye, they laughed at as a 'metaphor,' is the 'choice of the people.' This, every one must remember, was the corner stone of the creed of Price, Paine, O'Connor, and all their disciples; ... it is by no means strange that such a person [that is, Sheridan] should, for the sake of inculcating the doctrine of cashiering kings, sacrifice all dramatic propriety of character; but, it is strange, that the ambiguous applause of the galleries, and the corrupt praises of the newspapers, should ever have made pass for loyalty, those principles, which, if acted upon, would compel his Majesty's successors to ascend the throne, if they ascended it at all, from the hustings of Covent Garden, or of some other place, where 'the *choice of the people*' might be made known: that this should pass for attachment to the king and his royal progeny is, indeed, a most shocking proof of the national cullibility.[19]

This is likely to seem little short of paranoiac to us. Certainly it does not represent the response of the first audience to the play. We may be sure, on the showing of the reviews in the daily newspapers, that most of those who saw *Pizarro*, Tories as well as Whigs, were not disturbed by the political themes of the play. But if the intensity of their responses was excessive, Cobbett and the critic writing in *The Anti-Jacobin Review and Magazine* were not mistaken in detecting, beneath Sheridan's patriotic call for loyalty in the face of a dangerous enemy, an exposition of the political philosophy of the Opposition to Pitt. Sheridan was a monarchist, but he was also a Whig, one who on most though not all issues agreed with Fox. In his choice of his literary source, as in his own additions to it, Sheridan adhered to the political principles that had long guided his Parliamentary career. He provided a fable about the injustice of political oppression and colonial exploitation, and William Cobbett and William Pitt knew that he had done so.

Sheridan's years in Parliament had not destroyed his sense of the theatre. He chose precisely the height of the vogue of German drama to present his own adaptation from Kotzebue,[20] and he chose a play that permitted the fullest exploitation of the resources for stage spectacle of the recently rebuilt Drury Lane Theatre. Even from *The Rivals* in 1775 he had been a dramatist intensely preoccupied with the visual dimension of his plays, planning physical action as a reinforcement of his dialogue. And in staging *Pizarro* he could take advantage of the skills as acting manager of John Philip Kemble, a major innovator in scene design. He made good use as well of the company's musicians. Like *The Duenna* of a generation before, the play included songs, and it was performed with intervals of music. About half the music, Roger Fiske explains, is 'in Act II, scene ii, "The Temple of the Sun", which is operatic in emphasis'.[21] With all this, and with a cast which included John Philip Kemble, Charles Kemble, Mrs. Siddons, and Mrs. Jordan, it is scarcely surprising that the play succeeded.

The play in fact succeeded overwhelmingly. 'The joint reputation of Sheridan and Kotzebue,' *The Times* reported on 25 May 1799, 'and the first dramatic attempt of the former, after an interval of twenty years, attracted last night to the representation of *Pizarro*, as splendid and numerous an Audience as has ever been assembled at this House on any previous occasion.' In its first performances the play was too long and the elaborate stage machinery was handled with some awkwardness, but these defects were soon corrected and the play continued in a triumphant run. The success was no doubt enhanced by the fame of Sheridan and Kotzebue, but the records of performance assure us that the audiences encountered a most remarkable entertainment.

It was an entertainment conditioned by the physical structure of the new Drury Lane Theatre. Rebuilt in 1794, Drury Lane had been enlarged from its earlier ample proportions to accommodate over 3,600 persons.[22] It had become an immense structure, and its magnificence notwithstanding, its size made more difficult the portrayal of subtle interrelationships of characters and encouraged a declamatory style of acting and the use of spectacle. The audience could at least see what was happening on stage if some of them had trouble in hearing those actors or actresses, such as Mrs. Siddons, who could not without straining their voices speak loud enough to be heard by all. Mrs. Siddons's brother, John Philip Kemble, could make himself heard; the strength of his voice and his style of delivery were major assets in the new theatre. We can be sure that in writing those speeches of Rolla which sound like addresses to the House of Commons Sheridan took account of the abilities of Kemble as well as the nature of the theatre.

The opportunities for spectacle had been greatly enhanced. Kemble in his role as manager made important changes in scene design. Departing from the earlier exclusive reliance on painted scenery, Kemble in the new theatre, C. B. Hogan has explained,

> undertook . . . the actual construction of buildings with towers, battlements, drawbridges, archways. He used them in *Richard III*, in *Macbeth*, in *Pizarro*, in *Lodoiska*, in *Blue-Beard*, and in other pieces. These scenes he would place not invariably fronting the audience, but sometimes at an angle on the stage, or indeed at one side of it. Working with his principal scene designer, William Capon, he insisted upon exact archaeogical detail. . . .[23]

The care that Kemble took with the stage settings of *Pizarro* is suggested by a brief announcement in *The Times*, 23 May 1799, that the preparations 'for the Scenery of the new Play, prevents any Performance at this Theatre this Evening'.

What the audience saw on stage the following evening may be surmised from the printed stage directions and from the newspaper reviews, nearly all of which comment on the spectacle provided. The scenery, reports *The True Briton*, 25 May, 'is highly magnificent. The *Tent of Pizarro*, the *Temple of the Sun*, various views of a romantic country, the forest illuminated by the fiery element, and the subterranean retreat, are admirable achievements of the pencil.' '*A magnificent Pavilion near* PIZARRO's *Tent*—,' we read in the stage directions at the beginning of the first Act, '*a View of the Spanish Camp in the back Ground.*' *The Times*, 25 May, had warm praise: '*Pizarro's* Pavilion, and the Temple of the Sun are equal in point of brilliant effect to the best scenes of any of our Theatres; and the machinery, decorations, and dresses were marked with appropriate taste and splendour.' The 'machinery'— meaning the movable stage properties required for such a scene as Rolla's running over a suspended bridge and dropping it after himself—was in fact so complicated that it could not be handled expertly on the first night. 'It was the intention of the Managers,' reports *The True Briton*, 27 May, 'to postpone the second representation of *Pizarro* till Monday, that the scenery might be managed with more practised effect. . . .' But they changed their minds and performed the play—shortened by about half an hour—as planned; and by the fourth performance, *The Times* reported, 29 May, the machinery was handled with more ease. The stage directions of II.ii are reminiscent of some in Dryden and Howard's *The Indian Queen* of the seventeenth-century: '*The Temple of the Sun: it represents the magnificence of Peruvian idolatry. . . . A solemn march.*' *Pizarro* is in fact akin to the seventeenth-century heroic plays in its exotic scenery and ceremonial, though the new Drury Lane Theatre permitted much more striking effects than had been possible in the preceding century, when actors spoke before painted flats.

Horace Walpole had said of *The School for Scandal* that more parts were well acted in it than in any other play he could remember. A member of the first audiences of *Pizarro* could scarcely have said the same about that play, but to judge by the reports in the newspapers he would have found much to admire. Although doubts were expressed about the casting of Mrs. Jordan as Cora and Mrs. Siddons as Elvira,[24] the actors' performances—and above all that of Kemble—were praised. 'Kemble's *Rolla* takes the lead in animation, dignity, and pathos,' the critic for *The Times* wrote, 25 May, 'and is alone sufficient to confer popularity on the piece.' Sheridan knew the special abilities of the actors from long and close association, and he could take theatrical risks, knowing that they could render impressive what otherwise might seem absurd. Sheridan could scarcely have included the passages which sound like his speeches in Parliament had the Kembles not been leading members of the Drury Lane company.

It is not coincidence that *Pizarro* required a style of acting in which the Kembles excelled: declamatory delivery and formal, even statuesque gestures. One has but to remember Sir Thomas Lawrence's portrait of 'John Philip Kemble as Hamlet' and Sir Joshua Reynolds' of 'Mrs. Siddons as the Tragic Muse' to imagine their contribution to Sheridan's tragedy. Alan S. Downer has suggested the appropriateness of their styles of acting to *Pizzaro*. 'Her acting,' Mr. Downer writes about Sarah Siddons,

> was in the manner of Quin and Barton Booth, somewhat modified by the naturalism of Garrick. 'The quality of abstraction,' she said, 'has always appeared to me to be so necessary in the art of acting.' Her brother, John Philip Kemble, is usually described as an actor of classic dignity and little else, and

Macready remembered the 'grand deportment' of Mrs. Siddons. But this was the period when melodrama and romantic drama were once more coming into popularity, and the manners of Cato could not very convincingly be adopted by Rolla.[25]

Mrs. Siddons' comment about 'the quality of abstraction' seems curiously apt if we apply it to this play, in which personalities and moral and political issues have a kind of schematic simplicity, removed from complicating ambiguities. The closest approach to a credible character of mixed motives is that portrayed by Mrs. Siddons herself: Elvira, the mistress of Pizarro, who aids his enemies when she has learned the full extent of his depravity. But neither Elvira nor any other character in the play can be regarded as much more than an 'abstraction.'

The characters are intense and passionate, and except for Pizarro and his followers they have a near perfection of disinterested nobility. Pizarro himself is a static figure: as the critic writing in *The True Briton*, 25 May 1799, put it, he 'is a kind of *bugbear* that has little to do, except with the terror of his name'. But the terror of his name, supported by his formidable army, provides the needed test of the moral qualities of the protagonist, Rolla. Himself one of the Peruvian commanders, Rolla has loved and still loves Cora, who years earlier rejected him for Alonzo, the other commander. The second act opens with Alonzo, Cora, and their small son in an idyllic domestic scene placed in a wild terrain. Alonzo is called to arms, and in the battle with the Spaniards he is captured. Rolla rescues him by a strategem familiar in literature, best known to us in the variant Dickens used in *A Tale of Two Cities*: he persuades Alonzo to let him take his place in captivity with the threat that he will otherwise remain and die with him. Rolla is subsequently freed only to be faced with another self-imposed obligation to Cora: that of rescuing her kidnapped baby from the Spaniards. This he accomplishes in a scene that Kemble made famous, crossing a suspended bridge carrying the baby, and, to cut off pursuit, dropping the bridge after himself. The Spaniards cannot catch him, but they wound him with gunshot. He survives just long enough to return the baby to Cora, reassuring her when she sees blood upon her son with his dying words: ' "Tis my blood, Cora!" '

All this seems embarrassing in the last play of a writer of genius.

Critics were not wanting from the first night of performance who recognized its weakness. On 25 May the critic for *The Times* wrote that Sheridan had 'attempted a production with the boldness and extent of which he does not appear to have been sufficiently impressed'. Accurate understatement of the kind we would expect of *The Times*. Yet Sheridan brought it off with triumphant financial success. He seized a moment in theatrical history, exploiting the short-lived vogue of Kotzebue and bringing the talents of splendid actors to bear in a tragedy that could be interpreted as a commentary on urgent political issues. We cannot hear Kemble declaim the warnings about absolutist aggression, and without extended reading in eighteenth-century history we cannot understand the allusions to national issues that had engaged Sheridan in the House of Commons. What were assets in the first performances—the declamatory quality of the dialogue and the topical allusions—have become liabilities. Like so much else in Sheridan's career, *Pizarro* is anticlimactic.

Sheridan lived too long. The record of his career after the financial disaster of the Drury Lane fire in 1809 and his loss of his seat in Parliament in 1812 is chilling, and it casts a retrospective pall over his earlier political triumphs. He had drunk deeply and lived beyond his means long before 1809, but so had his Parliamentary betters Pitt and Fox, both of whom had the good fortune to die in middle age, Pitt at forty-six, Fox at fifty-seven. We are inclined to regard the personal irregularities of those two men—of Fox more than Pitt, for there are more irregularities to take into account—as the humanizing foibles of the great. Not so with Sheridan, whose later career has a disquieting resemblance to a cautionary moral fable. His political prominence was incomparably less than Pitt's, and it was less than Fox's, but he came to the edge of high office in the Regency Crisis, and for years before and after that anomalous—and for Sheridan frustrating—episode he was one of the most powerful orators in the House of Commons. He was furthermore a spokesman for causes which in the retrospect of the twentieth century seem just ones: regulation of English exploitation of India, conciliation with France when it was militarily possible, Parliamentary reform, emancipation of the Catholics, abolition of the Slave Trade. He was an eloquent spokesman for humanitarian causes in an oppressive age. And yet we remember him as 'poor Shery', a dissipated bankrupt and object of pity.

Pizarro came seventeen years before his death and ten years before his major financial and political reverses. It is anticlimactic but not because he had lost his powers. An effort of the left hand, it is perhaps to be regarded as hack work. Yet it is of a piece with his career: his Parliamentary as well as his dramatic career. He wrote as a propagandist for humanitarian causes. Pitt was of course right about the play: Sheridan had said it all before in his speeches. He wrote in his own style of Parliamentary oratory, too florid a style for our tastes, and he oversimplified issues. Yet he knew the resources of his stage, he knew the capabilities of his actors and musicians, he knew the taste of his audience—and he reached his limited objective of theatrical success.

Notes

CHAPTER 1

1. *The Dramatic Works of Richard Brinsley Sheridan* (ed. Cecil Price, Oxford, 1973).
2. *The Letters of Richard Brinsley Sheridan* (ed. Cecil Price, Oxford, 1966).
3. It may be an indication of the limitations on our literary taste imposed by the era in which we were educated that one of the few recent laudatory essays about *The School for Scandal* was written by an eminent scholar born late in the nineteenth century: Arthur C. Sprague, 'In Defence of a Masterpiece: "The School for Scandal" Re-examined,' in *English Studies Today*, 3rd Series (ed. G. E. Duthie, Edinburgh, 1964), pp. 125–35. Noting the decline in the reputation of the play with critics, Mr. Sprague praises it as 'a great acting play'.
   Sheridan has not been totally without admirers among younger scholars, though a distinction should perhaps be made between praise of *The Critic*, a farcical burlesque compatible with recent emphases in literary studies, and praise of the full-length comedies: cf. Samuel L. Macey, 'Sheridan: The Last of the Great Theatrical Satirists,' *Restoration and 18th Century Theatre Research*, ix (November 1970), 35–45; Philip K. Jason, 'A Twentieth-Century Response to *The Critic*,' *Theatre Survey*, xv (1974), 51–8. *The Rivals* has recently been the subject of a valuable essay, though one with a focus on the intersection of textual and theatrical history: Mark S. Auburn, 'The Pleasures of Sheridan's *The Rivals*: A Critical Study in the Light of Stage History,' *Modern Philology*, lxxii (1975), 256–71.
4. *Boswell's Life of Johnson* (ed. G. Birkbeck-Hill, rev. L. F. Powell, Oxford, 1934), iii, 116.
5. *Memoirs of the Life of John Philip Kemble, Esq.* (London, 1825), i, xi. Arthur Murphy had earlier written in more detail about Garrick's admiration for *The School for Scandal*. At Sheridan's request 'Garrick read the play with

close attention, and spoke of it in all companies with the highest appro-
bation. He attended the rehearsals, and was never known, on any former
occasion, to be more anxious for a favourite piece. He was proud of the new
manager, and, in a truimphant manner, boasted of the genius, to whom he
had consigned the conduct of the theatre' (*The Life of David Garrick, Esq.*
[London, 1801], ii, 144–5).

6. Quoted from *Dramatic Works* (ed. Price), p. 324.

7. Irving made the statement to W. Fraser Rae. In Rae, *Sheridan, A Biography*
(London, 1896), ii, 322.

8. *The Major Dramas of Richard Brinsley Sheridan* (ed. Nettleton, Boston,
1906); Nettleton, *English Drama of the Restoration and Eighteenth Century*
(New York, 1914); *British Dramatists from Dryden to Sheridan* (ed. Nettleton
and A. E. Case, Boston, 1939).

9. *The London Stage*, Pt. 5, *1776–1800* (ed. C. B. Hogan, Carbondale, Ill.,
1968), pp. clxxi–clxxiii.

10. The essay was published in *English Stage Comedy* (ed. W. K. Wimsatt, Jr.,
New York, 1955), pp. 98–125.

11. Ajodhia Nath Kaul, *The Action of English Comedy: Studies in the Encounter of
Abstraction and Experience from Shakespeare to Shaw* (New Haven, Conn.,
1970), pp. 131–49.

12. 'Goldsmith and Sheridan and the Supposed Revolution of "Laughing"
Against "Sentimental" Comedy,' in *Studies in Change and Revolution:
Aspects of English Intellectual History, 1640–1800* (ed. P. J. Korshin, Menston,
Yorkshire, 1972), pp. 237–76. Mr. Hume's essay was published after Mr.
Kaul's book. For references to earlier works supporting conclusions similar
to Mr. Hume's, see Chapter 2 and accompanying notes.

13. The first definition of the noun *burlesque* provided by the *Oxford English
Dictionary* is relevant to Sheridan's work: 'that species of literary composition, or of dramatic representation, which aims at exciting laughter by
caricature of the manner or spirit of serious works, or by ludicrous treatment of their subjects. . .'. The 'ludicrous treatment' of the subjects of
earlier dramatists, as well as of situations and techniques used in their plays,
is abundantly apparent in Sheridan. Insofar as his employment of 'burlesque'
is in intention critical—either of earlier drama or of the human experience
that provides its subject—it should be regarded as 'satirical.'

14. *Memoirs of . . . Kemble*, i, xi.

15. Cf. *The Morning Chronicle, and London Advertiser*, 22 November 1775.
After remarking that 'The fable of the *Duenna* is infinitely more substantial
than that of any other musical performance we remember,' the reviewer
writes that 'The story of it greatly resembles the story of a Spanish Play, to
be met with in a collection of French translations of Theatrical Pieces,
entitled Le Thèatre Espagnol. . .' I. consider this subject below, pp. 65–6.

16. Cf. John Loftis, 'Dryden's Comedies,' in *John Dryden* (ed. E. R. Miner, London, 1972), pp. 42–3.
17. *The First Modern Comedies: The Significance of Etherege, Wycherley and Congreve* (Cambridge, Mass., 1959).
18. It suggests much about Sheridan's stylistic ideals that Dryden was his favorite poet and that, like Dryden and Samuel Johnson—and many others in the century that separated those two—Sheridan hated puns: *Reminiscences of Michael Kelly* (London, 1826), ii, 348, 357–8.
19. See below, p. 14.
20. Arthur Sherbo, *English Sentimental Drama* (East Lansing, Mich., 1957), pp. 1–14. For an analysis of theoretical problems presented by the phenomenon of 'sentimentalism,' see Calhoun Winton, 'Sentimentalism and Theater Reform in the Early Eighteenth Century,' in *Quick Springs of Sense: Studies in the Eighteenth Century* (ed. L. S. Champion, Athens, Georgia, 1974), pp. 97–112.

CHAPTER 2

1. *Memoirs of the Life of David Garrick, Esq.* (London, 1780), ii, 331.
2. 'Aspects of Sentimentalism in Eighteenth-Century Literature,' in *The Augustan Milieu* (ed. H. K. Miller, E. Rothstein, and G. S. Rousseau, Oxford, 1970), p. 252.
3. Arthur Sherbo, *English Sentimental Drama* (East Lansing, Mich., 1957), *passim*; Hume, 'Goldsmith and Sheridan', *loc. cit.*
4. Oliver W. Ferguson, 'Sir Fretful Plagiary and Goldsmith's "An Essay on the Theatre," ' in *Quick Springs of Sense* (ed. L. S. Champion), pp. 113–20.
5. Stanley T. Williams, *Richard Cumberland: His Life and Dramatic Works* (New Haven, Conn., 1917), p. 111.
6. *The Collected Works of Oliver Goldsmith* (ed. Arthur Friedman, Oxford, 1966), iv, 355–6. Subsequent quotations from Goldsmith are based on this edition.
7. *Memoirs of Richard Cumberland, Written by Himself* (London, 1806), p. 271.
8. Cf. Williams, *Cumberland*, pp. 126ff.; Ricardo Quintana, *Oliver Goldsmith: A Georgian Study* (New York, 1967), p. 169. I am not convinced by Mr. Ferguson's argument that Cumberland's vanity prevented him from perceiving the irony in Goldsmith's lines: Ferguson, *op. cit.*
9. *The Plays of Richard Steele* (ed. Shirley Strum Kenny, Oxford, 1971), pp. 283–4.
10. Preface to Shakespeare in *Johnson on Shakespeare* (ed. Arthur Sherbo, New Haven, Conn., 1968) in *Works*, vii, 88.

11. Allardyce Nicoll, *A History of English Drama, 1660–1900* (Cambridge, Eng., 1955), iii, 158, comments on this passage.

12. Mark Schorer, 'Hugh Kelly: His Place in the Sentimental School,' *Philological Quarterly*, xii (1933), 389–401.

13. *The British Theatre* (London, 1808), xii, in 'Remarks' prefixed to the play, pp. 5–6.

14. Elizabeth P. Stein, *David Garrick, Dramatist* (New York, 1938), p. 202.

15. K. A. Burnim, *David Garrick, Director* (Pittsburgh, Pa., 1961), p. 11.

16. Nicoll, *History of English Drama*, iii, 117. Andrew Schiller perceptively notes that *The School for Scandal*, in its moral dimension, resembles Molière more closely than Congreve: '*The School for Scandal*: The Restoration Unrestored,' *PMLA*, lxxi (1956), 698.

17. *Memoirs of . . . Garrick*, ii, 122.

18. A critic writing in the *St. James's Chronicle* noted that Garrick had destroyed the force of the play by his changes: Charles Harold Gray, *Theatrical Criticism in London to 1795* (New York, 1931), p. 198.

19. Steele, *The Conscious Lovers* (ed. Shirley Strum Kenny, Lincoln, Neb., 1968), p. xvi.

20. Steele, *Plays* (ed. Kenny), pp. 284–90.

21. Theodore G. Grieder, Jr., 'The French Revolution in the British Drama: A Study in British Popular Literature of the Decade of Revolution' (unpubl. diss., Stanford University, 1957). For Sheridan's allusions in *Pizarro*, 1799, to the war with France, see below, pp. 125–6; 131–3.

22. Letter to Samuel Whitbread, 7 March 1815, in *Letters* (ed. Price), iii, 220.

23. *Speeches of . . . Richard Brinsley Sheridan*. 'Edited by a Constitutional Friend.' (London, 1816), iv, 188–9.

24. In his prologue to *The Critic*, the Honorable Richard Fitzpatrick expresses regret that the reaction from the permissiveness of Restoration comedy on sexual subjects has been excessive.

25. Cf. Harry William Pedicord, *The Theatrical Public in the Time of Garrick* (New York, 1954), and Leo Hughes, *The Drama's Patrons: A Study of the Eighteenth-Century London Audience* (Austin, Texas, 1971).

26. *The London Stage*, Pt. 4, *1747–1776* (Carbondale, Ill., 1962), p. clxix. In a recent study of the mid-century repertory, Cecil Price has used the resources provided by *The London Stage* to advantage: *Theatre in the Age of Garrick* (Oxford, 1973), pp. 142–74.

27. Davies, *Memoirs . . . of Garrick*, ii, 142ff., refers to Goldsmith's 'attack' on Garrick.

28. *The London Stage*, Pt. 4, *1747–1776*, pp. clxiiff.

CHAPTER 3

1. *Boswell's Life of Johnson* (ed. G. Birkbeck-Hill), iii, 116.
2. *Lectures on the English Comic Writers* (London, 1819), pp. 336–7.
3. A remark by Mr. Dangle in *The Critic* (III.i) aptly expresses Sheridan's sensitivity to the visual dimension of his plays: 'Ah! there certainly is a vast deal to be done on the stage by dumb shew, and expression of face, and a judicious author knows how much he may trust to it.'
4. *Memoirs of . . . Mrs. Frances Sheridan* (London, 1824), p. 406.
5. Sichel, *Sheridan*, i, 505.
6. Cf. *Dramatic Works* (ed. Price), pp. 37–8. *A Journey to Bath* was printed in *Sheridan's Plays now printed as he wrote them and his Mother's unpublished Comedy . . .* (ed. W. Fraser Rae, London, 1902), pp. 263–318.
7. Cf. H. J. Habakkuk, 'Marriage Settlements in the Eighteenth Century,' in *Transactions* of the Royal Historical Society, 4th Series, xxiii (1950), 24. Habakkuk is primarily concerned with the early eighteenth century.
8. Introduction to Clementina Black, *The Linleys of Bath* (New York, 1926), p. viii.
9. Price writes that Long was fifty-nine in 1771: *Dramatic Works*, p. 287. John Genest, who writes as though he had personal knowledge of the individuals involved in the episode, says 'Flint' (i.e., Walter Long) in Samuel Foote's *The Maid of Bath* (1771) died in 1807: [Genest], *Some Account of the English Stage* (Bath, 1832), v, 313. If both Genest and Price are correct, Long lived to be ninety-five.
10. For an authoritative analysis of conflicting interpretations of the matter, see Cecil Price, 'Hymen and Hirco: A Vision', *Times Literary Supplement*, 11 July 1958, p. 396. Cf. also, Price, 'Sheridan-Linley Documents', *Theatre Notebook*, xxi (1967), 165–6.
11. *Dramatic Works* (ed. Price), p. 70.
12. *Ibid.*, pp. 38–9.
13. *The Tender Husband* held the stage into Sheridan's time, though by 1775 its popularity had waned: Steele, *Plays* (ed. Kenny), pp. 198–9. That *The Tender Husband* was still known to theatre-goers is implied by a remark of a critic writing in *The Morning Chronicle*, 18 January 1775, who refers to Steele's play by its second title: 'The romantic vein of *Lydia Languish* is not so well imagined, or so ably sustained as Steele's Lady (we forget her name) in the *Accomplished Fools*. . .'.
14. *Eighteenth-Century Drama: Afterpieces* (ed. R. W. Bevis, London, 1970), p. 136.
15. Miriam Gabriel and Paul Mueschke, 'Two Contemporary Sources of Sheridan's *The Rivals*,' *PMLA*, xliii (1928), 237–50.

16. Tuvia Bloch, 'The Antecedents of Sheridan's Faulkland,' *Philological Quarterly*, xlix (1970), 266–7.
17. His older sister, Alicia Lefanu, wrote in 1817 about the incident to Lady Sydney Morgan, who quoted from Alicia's letter in her own *Memoirs* (London, 1863), ii, 61. Cf. *The Rivals* (ed. Richard L. Purdy, Oxford, 1935), p. xxxiii.
18. *The Late Augustans* (ed. Donald Davie, London, 1958), p. xiv.
19. *Memoirs of the Life of the Right Honourable Richard Brinsley Sheridan* (London, 1825), p. 104.
20. A more critical appraisal of Faulkland and Julia appears in *The Morning Chronicle*, 18 January 1775 (quoted in *The Plays and Poems of Richard Brinsley Sheridan* [ed. R. Crompton Rhodes, Oxford, 1928], i, 120).
21. Quoted from *Plays and Poems* (ed. Rhodes), i, 123–4.
22. Cf. *The Rivals* (ed. Purdy), pp. xvii–xx.
23. J. O. Bartley, *Teague, Shenkin and Sawney* (Cork, 1954), p. 183.
24. *Boswell's Life of Johnson* (ed. G. B. Hill), ii, 369.
25. His niece, Alicia Lefanu, wrote that he had suffered in his youth from gossip: *Memoirs of . . . Mrs. Frances Sheridan*, p. 406.
26. Sichel, *Sheridan*, i, 489.
27. She died 18 January 1820 and was buried in the churchyard of St. Paul's, Covent Garden, where an inscription commemorates her: Black, *The Linleys*, p. 276.
28. *Some Account of the English Stage*, v, 312–13.
29. Cf. Simon Trefman, *Sam. Foote, Comedian, 1720–1777* (New York, 1971), pp. 279–82. Trefman (pp. 233–4) describes a possible reference to Sheridan and Elizabeth's elopement in Foote's *A Trip to Calais* (1776).
30. *Letters* (ed. Price), i, 85.
31. Cf. *The Rivals* (ed. Purdy), pp. xii–xiv.
32. *Ibid.*, pp. xlvii–xlix.
33. In the two centuries *The Rivals* has held the stage, episodes and characters have in fact often been excised in performance: Auburn, 'The Pleasures of Sheridan's *The Rivals*,' *loc cit.*
34. *Plays and Poems* (ed. Rhodes), i, 248.
35. *Letters* (ed. Price), i, 88n. Roger Fiske writes that Thomas Linley the Younger 'was responsible for half the opera': *English Theatre Music in the Eighteenth Century* (London, 1973), p. 416.
36. *Letters* (ed. Price), i, 89.
37. C. H. Gray, *Theatrical Criticism in London*, p. 276.
38. [William Smyth], *Memoir of Mr. Sheridan* (Leeds, 1840), p. 6, as quoted in *Dramatic Works* (ed. Price), p. 214.
39. Cf. John Loftis, *The Spanish Plays of Neoclassical England* (New Haven, Conn., 1973), *passim*.

40. Peter A. Tasch, *The Dramatic Cobbler: The Life and Works of Isaac Bickerstaff* (Lewisburg, Penna., 1971), pp. 198–207.
41. Loftis, *Spanish Plays*, pp. 91–5.
42. It is illustrative of Dibdin's zeal in searching for literary 'sources' of Sheridan's play that he refers to an incident in *The Rivals* (presumably that in which Faulkland falsely tells Julia he must flee the country [V.i]) as derived from the fifteenth-century poem, 'The Nut-Brown Maid': *The Musical Tour* (Sheffield, 1788), p. 259.
43. Dibdin, *Musical Tour*, p. 260.
44. *Ibid.*, pp. 413–14. I would guess he would have been aware that unflattering comparisons between his own opera and Sheridan's would have been made had he mentioned the latter.
45. John Wilson Bowyer, *The Celebrated Mrs. Centlivre* (Durham, N.C., 1952), p. 177.
46. Sichel, *Sheridan*, i, 509.
47. Moore, *Sheridan*, pp. 128–9.
48. Cf. Sichel, *Sheridan*, i, 277–8, 507–9.
49. A writer in *The Morning Chronicle*, 27 November 1775, described the damaging consequences for Garrick at Drury Lane of the popularity of *The Duenna*: 'He [Garrick] himself performs his best parts three or four times a week; and yet this new sing song thing, the Duenna, brings crowded houses to Covent Garden, and leaves Roscius almost in utter solitude."
50. After election to Parliament, Sheridan was notably liberal in his advocacy of legislation intended to provide greater freedom for Catholics: cf. Sichel, *Sheridan*, i, 117–19; ii, 324.
51. John Loftis, *The Politics of Drama in Augustan England* (Oxford, 1963), pp. 94–9.
52. Cf. Bertrand H. Bronson, *Facets of the Enlightenment* (Berkeley, Calif., 1968), 'The Beggar's Opera,' pp. 86–8.
53. Quoted from Gray, *Theatrical Criticism*, p. 276.

CHAPTER 4

1. *The Formation of English Neo-Classical Thought* (Princeton, 1967).
2. 'What Indeed Was Neo-Classicism?', *Journal of British Studies*, x (November 1970), 69–79.
3. 'When Was Neoclassicism?', *Facets of the Enlightenment*, pp. 1–25.
4. *Dryden's Criticism* (Ithaca, N.Y., 1970), p. 175.
5. To be as specific as possible concerning the nature as well as the continuity of the comic theory I am calling neoclassical, I refer to assumptions about the genre of comedy, as it is differentiated from tragedy, that Aristotle

L

expresses or implies in his few brief remarks on the subject in *The Poetics*. With variations in emphasis, these assumptions are reiterated—sometimes expressed ironically, sometimes in direct exposition—by Dryden in 1668 through the character Lisideius in *Of Dramatick Poesie* (who more than Neander expresses received opinion on the subject), by Dryden in 1679 in incidental remarks in 'The Grounds of Criticism in Tragedy,' by Shadwell in 1671 in the preface to *The Humorists*, by Jeremy Collier in 1698 in *A Short View of the Immorality and Profaneness of the English Stage*, by John Dennis in 1698 in *The Usefulness of the Stage* and again in 1722 and 1723 in *A Defence of Sir Fopling Flutter, a Comedy*, and *Remarks on a Play, Call'd, The Conscious Lovers, a Comedy*, by Addison in 1711 in *The Spectator*, No. 249, by Henry Fielding in 1749 in *Tom Jones*, Book XII, Chapter 5, by Goldsmith in 1759 in *An Enquiry into the Present State of Polite Learning in Europe* and again in 1773 in his essay 'On the Theatre,' and by Sheridan in 1779 in *The Critic*.

6. *Facets of the Enlightenment*, p. 24.
7. '*Of Dramatic Poesy*' *and Other Critical Essays* (ed. George Watson, London, 1962), i, 58.
8. *Ibid.*, i, 279.
9. *Ibid.*, i, 152.
10. *Ibid.*, i, 25.
11. *Works* (ed. Earl Miner and V. A. Dearing, Berkeley, Calif., 1969), iii, 111.
12. '*Of Dramatic Poesy*' (ed. Watson), ii, 274, 293–4. However, in one of his poems he included in the *Fables*, 'Cymon and Iphigenia,' from Boccaccio. Dryden was more aggressive in his own defence: *The Poems and Fables of John Dryden* (ed. James Kinsley, London, 1962), pp. 815–16.
13. Quoted from *Dramatic Works* (ed. Price), p. 556.
14. I follow the first edition of 1697 in printing this passage as prose. However, some modern editors of the play, including the latest, Curt A. Zimansky (Lincoln, Neb., 1970, p. 134), print it as irregular verse.
15. *Dramatic Works* (ed. Price), pp. 293–5.
16. As in Kaul, *The Action of English Comedy*, pp. 137–8.
17. *Memoirs of the Public and Private Life of the Right Honorable Richard Brinsley Sheridan* (London, 1817), i, 157–9.
18. *Memoirs of . . . Mrs. Frances Sheridan*, pp. 407–8.
19. 'The Grounds of Criticism in Tragedy,' *Critical Essays* (ed. Watson), i, 243–4.
20. *Memoirs of . . . Kemble*, i, xii. Charles Dibdin made the more frequent comparison of Sheridan's play to *The Way of the World*, isolating in doing so, however, a resemblance between the plays that implies an interpretation of *The School for Scandal* as an acerbic satire: Sheridan's '*School* itself,' Dibdin

wrote, 'is CONGREVE's *Cabal*, and the play may fairly be called a sequel to *The Way of the World*' (*Musical Tour*, p. 260).

21. Thomas Moore reports that Sheridan denied having read Wycherley: *Memoirs of . . . Sheridan*, p. 188.

22. Cf. Rose A. Zimbardo, *Wycherley's Drama: A Link in the Development of English Satire* (New Haven, Conn., 1965), *passim*.

23. *Memoirs of . . . Sheridan*, i, 159–60.

24. Alicia Lefanu, *Memoirs of . . . Mrs. Frances Sheridan*, pp. 404–5.

25. Cf. '*The Way to Keep Him*' *and Five Other Plays by Arthur Murphy* (ed. John P. Emery, New York, 1956), p. 334.

26. They are concisely summarized in *Dramatic Works* (ed. Price), pp. 293–5.

27. Alicia Lefanu, *Memoirs of . . . Mrs. Frances Sheridan*, pp. 407–10.

28. *Memoirs of . . . Sheridan*, i, 165–6.

29. *Dramatic Works* (ed. Price), p. 293.

30. Sheridan did not himself prepare *The School for Scandal* for the press despite the publication during his lifetime of a number of unauthorized editions, some with very corrupt texts. Alicia Lefanu argued (*Memoirs of . . . Mrs. Frances Sheridan*, p. 411) that he did not do so because he wished 'to confine the performance of the play in London to his own theatre.' Yet a remark of Sheridan's recorded by Thomas Moore implies that Sheridan could never bring himself to regard the play as finished: Moore, *Memoirs, Journal, and Correspondence of Thomas Moore* (ed. Lord John Russell, London, 1853), ii, 302.

31. James Boaden, *Memoirs of . . . Kemble*, i, xiv.

32. For an authoritative account of this subject, see Stuart M. Tave, *The Amiable Humorist: A Study in the Comic Theory and Criticism of the Eighteenth and Early Nineteenth Centuries* (Chicago, 1960).

33. Moore, *Memoirs of . . . Sheridan*, p. 181.

34. Walpole to Robert Jephson, 13 July 1777, in *The Letters of Horace Walpole* (ed. Mrs. Paget Toynbee, Oxford, 1904) x, 82.

35. Quoted from *Dramatic Works* (ed. Price), p. 322.

36. For a study of the actors' interpretation of their roles, see Christian Deelman, 'The Original Cast of *The School for Scandal*,' *The Review of English Studies*, N.S. xiii (1962), 257–66.

37. *Memoirs of . . . Kemble*, i, 51.

38. *Ibid.*, i, 53–4.

39. *Ibid.*, i, 60–1.

40. Cf. *Dramatic Works* (ed. Price), pp. 304–5.

41. *Memoirs of . . . Kemble*, i, 83.

42. James Boaden, *The Life of Mrs. Jordan* (London, 1831), ii, 96. Cf. Kelly, *Reminiscences*, ii, 129–30.

CHAPTER 5

1. Kelly, *Reminiscences*, ii, 360.
2. *Ibid.*, ii, 246: 'He [Sheridan] dreaded the newspapers, and always courted their friendship.'
3. The absurd stories about Sheridan's theft of literary property persisted, to be repeated after his death by his hostile and inaccurate biographer, John Watkins. Cf. *Memoirs*, i, 160–1. 'He [Sheridan] could not be unacquainted with what was very commonly reported soon after the appearance of the play, for he has some broad allusions to the subject in the celebrated farce which he avowedly brought out for the purpose of making his detractors ridiculous. But contempt is no answer, and ridicule is no test of truth.'
4. Sichel, *Sheridan*, ii, 391; *Letters* (ed. Price), i, 116n.; *The London Stage, Pt. 5, 1776–1800* (ed. Hogan), pp. 192–3, 274, 451.
5. The distinction of the three persons Sheridan invited to hear a private reading of *The Critic* before its production at Drury Lane suggests the prominence he had already attained: the Honorable Richard Fitzpatrick (the author of the prologue), son of an earl; William Windham, later to be offered and to refuse a peerage; and General John Burgoyne, a former commander of British forces in America during the Revolution and himself a dramatist (*Letters* [ed. Price], i, 128–9).
6. For an account of the journalistic criticism of Sheridan, see C. H. Gray, *Theatrical Criticism in London, passim.*
7. John Loftis, *Steele at Drury Lane* (Berkeley, Calif., 1952), pp. 195–213.
8. For illuminating considerations of the history and theory of the stage burlesque (to which I am indebted), see Samuel L. Macey, 'Sheridan: The Last of the Great Theatrical Satirists,' *loc. cit.*; and Philip K. Jason, 'A Twentieth-Century Response to *The Critic*,' *loc. cit.*
9. *The Knight of the Burning Pestle* by Beaumont and Fletcher (New York, 1908).
10. *Burlesque Plays of the Eighteenth Century* (ed. Simon Trussler, London, 1969), p. 2.
11. *Dramatic Works* (ed. Price), p. 472.
12. Trussler, *op. cit.*, p. xii.
13. *Ibid.* It is worth noting that for all the generalized quality of its parody *The Critic* was not fully intelligible to its first audiences. Writing about the second and third acts, a contributor to *The Morning Chronicle*, 1 November 1779, attributed 'their want of effect' in part 'to the satire being too much concealed. . .'. The satire was not fully intelligible even to such a well-informed man as Horace Walpole: *The Yale Edition of Horace Walpole's*

Correspondence (ed. W. S. Lewis, New Haven, Conn., 1965), xxxiii, 159.

14. For accounts of these burlesques, see Dane Farnsworth Smith, *Plays About the Theatre in England from . . . 1671 to . . . 1737* (London, 1936); D. F. Smith, *The Critics in the Audience of the London Theatres From Buckingham to Sheridan* (Albuquerque, N.M., 1953); Victor C. Clinton-Baddeley, *The Burlesque Tradition in the English Theatre After 1660* (London, 1952); Macey, 'Sheridan: The Last of the Great Theatrical Satirists,' *loc. cit.*

15. For an account of the play and its reception in the theatre, see George Sherburn, 'The Fortunes and Misfortunes of *Three Hours After Marriage*,' *Modern Philology*, xxiv (August 1926), 91–109.

16. Moore, *Sheridan*, i, 13–16. Price reprints the fragment with commentary on the collaboration between Halhed and Sheridan and on the significance of the fragment for *The Critic: Dramatic Works* (ed. Price), pp. 793–6. Nettleton includes a discussion of 'Sheridan's *Jupiter*, A Forerunner of *The Critic*,': *Major Dramas*, pp. lxxxiii–lxxxvi.

17. P. T. Dircks, Introduction, [Kane O'Hara], *Midas: An English Burletta* (Los Angeles, The Augustan Reprint Society, 1974), pp. iii–viii.

18. F. W. Bateson, 'Notes on the Text of Two Sheridan Plays,' *Review of English Studies*, xvi (1940), 314–17; *Dramatic Works* (ed. Price), pp. 24–30.

19. Now in the Henry E. Huntington Library, San Marino, Calif.

20. Quoted from Bateson, *op. cit.*, p. 315.

21. On the identities of the persons who are the subjects of the caricatures, see *Major Dramas* (ed. Nettleton), pp. xciv–c; *Dramatic Works* (ed. Price), pp. 469–72.

22. For a comprehensive review of the subject, see Williams, *Richard Cumberland*, pp. 136–50.

23. *Dramatic Works* (ed. Price), p. 471.

24. *Kemble*, I, 63–4. We cannot know with assurance what Sheridan's motive was in assigning authorship to Puff. Mr. R. C. Rhodes suggests that the motive may be traced to a theatrical project of the actor Thomas King, the original Puff, who in August 1779 had produced at Sadler's Wells Theatre a pageant entitled *The Prophecy; or, Queen Elizabeth at Tilbury*, which had included a depiction of the defeat of the Spanish Armada. Perhaps in his assignment of the tragedy to Puff (i.e. King), Sheridan was playfully mocking one of his own actors. See *Poems and Plays* (ed. Rhodes), ii, 181–2. But whatever the workings of Sheridan's mind, I believe *The Critic* would have been damaged had the assault on Fretful (i.e. Cumberland) been continued for two more acts

25. Quoted from Williams, *Cumberland*, pp. 141–2.

26. Cf. *Dramatic Works* (ed. Price), p. 496.

27. A writer for *The Morning Chronicle*, 1 November 1779, objected to the

cruelty in the depiction of Sir Fretful: 'His [Parsons'] face expressed envy, malice, and arrogance, so powerfully, that we felt compassion for the devoted object of the satire, and could not help thinking Mr. Sheridan had mistaken cruelty for justice. . .'.

28. *Kemble*, i, 63.

29. For discussion of conflicting attitudes about literary property and plagiarism in the Restoration and eighteenth century, see John Loftis, Introduction, pp. ix-xiii, Gerard Langbaine, *An Account of the English Dramatick Poets* (Los Angeles, The Augustan Reprint Society, 1971).

30. Buckingham apparently wrote *The Rehearsal* with assistance from a group of collaborators. He began the play some eight years before its première: *British Dramatists from Dryden to Sheridan*, 2nd ed. (ed. Nettleton, Case, and Stone, New York, 1969), p. 39.

31. Sybil Rosenfeld, *A Short History of Scene Design in Great Britain* (Oxford, 1973), p. 91. De Loutherbourg provides Mr. Puff with one of his examples of 'the *puff direct*'. *The Critic*, I.ii: 'As to the scenery—The miraculous power of Mr. DE LOUTHERBOURG's pencil are universally acknowledged!'

32. Rosenfeld, *op. cit.*, pp. 90–3.

33. However, Sheridan may not have had the threatened invasion in mind when he began to write *The Critic*: cf. *Dramatic Works* (ed. Price), p. 467. Price describes Sheridan's satirical hits at the inadequate efforts to strengthen the nation's defences (p. 475), but he does not allude to what I take to be a personal reference to Lord North.

34. Navy Records Society *Publications*, Vol. 75, *The Private Papers of John, Earl of Sandwich . . . 1771–82* (London, 1936), iii, 20.

35. Nettleton cites a passage in Fielding's *The Historical Register for the Year 1736* as a possible source for the Burleigh episode: *Major Dramas*, p. lxxxix. In Fielding, Medley, like Puff commenting on the rehearsal of a play he has written, explains the silence of four 'Patriots' (i.e., opponents of Walpole) when they come on stage with the remark: "Sir, what they think now cannot well be spoke, but you may conjecture a great deal from their shaking their Heads.' Nettleton does not refer to Lord North. The resemblance of *The Critic* in this detail to *The Historical Register*, a political satire, would if anything strengthen the probability that Sheridan intended his episode as a sly criticism of Lord North.

36. Butterfield, *George III, Lord North, and the People, 1779–80* (London, 1949), pp. 41–53. On Lord North's state of mind, see also Richard Pares, *King George III and the Politicians* (Oxford, 1953), p. 161.

37. For comment on emotional nuances conveyed by Sheridan's concluding procession, see Clinton-Baddeley, *op, cit.*, pp. 77–9.

38. Alfred Thayer Mahan, *The Influence of Sea Power upon History, 1660–1783* (London, 1890), pp. 505ff.

CHAPTER 6

1. 17 February, 1783, in *Speeches of . . . Sheridan*, i, 47. See also Sichel, *Sheridan*, ii, 15.
2. Joseph W. Donohue, Jr., *Dramatic Character in the English Romantic Age* (Princeton, N.J., 1970), p. 139. In this chapter I am indebted to Mr. Donohue's discussion of *Pizarro* (pp. 125–56). I am indebted as well to R. Crompton Rhodes's commentary on the play in *Plays and Poems*, iii, 5–15, and to Cecil Price's in *Dramatic Works*, pp. 625–50.
3. It was praised, for example, in the newspaper *The True Briton*, the Tory bias of which is expressed in the epigraph printed below its title: '*Nolumus Leges Angliae Mutari.*'
4. Herschel Baker, *John Philip Kemble: The Actor in His Theatre* (Cambridge, Mass., 1942), pp. 232–3.
5. For an account of the translation, or translations, of the German play used by Sheridan, see *Dramatic Works* (ed. Price), pp. 645–6.
6. *Pizarro* (ed. W. Oxberry, London, 1824), p. viii: 'Pitt, having been to see the play, was asked by a friend his opinion of it. "If you mean (said he) what Sheridan has written, there is nothing new in it, for I heard it all long ago in his speeches at Hastings's trial."' John Watkins, Sheridan's early biographer, also commented on his borrowings from his Hastings speeches: *Memoirs*; ii, 292.
7. *Speeches of the Managers and Counsel in the Trial of Warren Hastings* (ed. A. E. Bond, London. 1859–61), i, 676; Sichel, *Sheridan*, ii, 162.
8. *Memoirs of . . . Sheridan*, p. 583.
9. Philip Anthony Brown, *The French Revolution in English History* (London, 1918), *passim*.
10. Sheridan, *Speeches*, ii, 291.
11. Sichel, *Sheridan*, ii, 140.
12. *The Morning Post*, 31 May 1799. Cited in *Dramatic Works* (ed. Price), p. 635.
13. See Michael T. H. Sadleir, *The Political Career of Richard Brinsley Sheridan* (Oxford, 1912), pp. 71–3.
14. Sheridan, *Speeches*, iv, 468.
15. *Ibid.*, iv, 471.
16. *Dramatic Works* (ed. Price), pp. 788–90.
17. *Poetry of the 'Anti-Jacobin'* (ed. L. Rice-Oxley, Oxford, 1924), p. 130.
18. Donohue, *op. cit.*, pp. 147, 148–9, comments on the criticism of *Pizarro* in the *Anti-Jacobin Review and Magazine*.
19. *The Political Proteus* (London, 1804), pp. 84–5.
20. Frank Woodyer Stokoe, *German Influence in the English Romantic Period, 1788–1818* (New York, 1963), pp. 48–9: 'The enthusiasm for Kotzebue and

all his works reaches its maniacal climax in 1799, in which year I count twenty-seven translations or adaptations from Kotzebue, and there may well have been more.'

21. *English Theatre Music in the Eighteenth Century*, p. 575. Fiske provides a comprehensive account of the music performed in *Pizarro*.

22. *The London Stage, Pt. 5, 1776–1800* (ed. Hogan), pp. xlii–xliv.

23. *Ibid.*, p. lxiv. See also Russell Thomas, 'Contemporary Taste in the Stage Decorations of London Theaters, 1770–1800,' *Modern Philology*, xlii (Nov. 1944), 65–78.

24. *The Times*, 25 May 1799.

25. 'Nature to Advantage Dressed: Eighteenth-Century Acting,' *PMLA*, lviii (1943), 1017.

Chronology

1751   Sheridan born in Dublin in the autumn (precise date unknown), son of Thomas Sheridan, an actor and teacher of elocution, and his wife Frances, a novelist and playwright. Grandson of Thomas Sheridan, D.D., a friend of Jonathan Swift.

1754   Elizabeth Ann Linley, later Sheridan's first wife, born at Bath, probably in September, the daughter of Thomas Linley, a musician and composer, and his wife Mary.

1762–
c. 1768 Sheridan attends Harrow school.

1766   Death of Sheridan's mother, 22 September.

1770   The Sheridan family takes up residence at Bath, where Thomas Sheridan establishes an academy of oratory. At the instigation of her parents, Elizabeth Linley betrothed to Walter Long, a wealthy but elderly man. Betrothal subsequently broken off, with a large financial settlement on Elizabeth by Long.

1771   Performance at the Little Theatre in the Haymarket of Samuel Foote's *The Maid of Bath*, a farcical rendering in transparent allegory of Elizabeth Linley's relations with Walter Long and also with another unwelcome suitor.

1772   Sheridan escorts Elizabeth Linley to France so that she can escape the embarrassing advances of Thomas Mathews, a married man. Upon returning to England, Sheridan fights two duels with Mathews, in the second of which Sheridan suffers a near-fatal wound.

1773   Sheridan and Elizabeth are married, 13 April, against the wishes of both their fathers. They settle in London.

1775   *The Rivals* performed at Covent Garden, 17 January, with little success. Withdrawn, revised, and performed again, 28 January, this time successfully. Sheridan's reputation established when his comic opera, *The Duenna*, has a run of seventy-five performances at Covent Garden, beginning 21 November.

1776   Upon the retirement of David Garrick, Sheridan in partnership with his father-in-law and a physician gains control of Drury Lane Theatre.

1777   *A Trip to Scarborough*, an adaptation of Vanbrugh's *The Relapse*, first performed, 24 February. On the nomination of Samuel Johnson, elected a member of The Club, 14 March. *The School for Scandal* begins a brilliant run, 8 May.

1779   *The Critic* first performed, 30 October.

1780   Elected to Parliament for Stafford, 12 September. Remainder of career primarily devoted to public affairs.

1782   Under-Secretary of State for Foreign Affairs.

1783   Secretary to the Treasury.

1787   Already known for his skill in debate, establishes a great reputation for oratory in a speech in the House of Commons, 7 February, in the impeachment of Warren Hastings.

1788   Enhances his reputation for oratory with other speeches in June during the trial of Hastings in Westminster Hall.
Death of his father, August.
During the Regency Crisis, November and December, an advisor to the Prince of Wales.

1792   Death of Elizabeth Sheridan, 28 June.

1794   Completion of the rebuilding of Drury Lane Theatre.

1795   Marries Ester Ogle, daughter of the Dean of Winchester Cathedral, 27 April.

1799   *Pizarro* begins a long and financially-successful run, 24 May.

1806–7   Serves in the Ministry of 'All the Talents' as Treasurer of the Navy.

1806   Upon the death of Charles James Fox, Sheridan succeeds him as Member of Parliament for Westminster.

1807   Fails to win election for Westminster but remains in the House of Commons as Member for Ilchester.

1809   Drury Lane Theatre burns, 24 February, with grave financial consequences for Sheridan.

1812   Loses his seat in the House of Commons.

1813   Arrested for debt.

1816   Death, 7 July. Buried in Poet's Corner, Westminster Abbey.

Select Bibliography

(I) EDITIONS

The standard edition of *The Dramatic Works of Richard Brinsley Sheridan* is now and will remain in the predictable future that of Cecil Price (1973). Several older editions are useful for special reasons: that of R. Crompton Rhodes (1928) because of the critical commentary provided, some of it written by the editor and some of it quoted from contemporaries of Sheridan; and that by W. Fraser Rae (1902) because it prints some of the plays in texts that antedate the final revisions of them, and also because it includes *A Journey to London*, a fragment of a comedy written by Sheridan's mother from which he apparently took suggestions for *The Rivals*. George Henry Nettleton's *The Major Dramas of Richard Brinsley Sheridan* (1906), which includes only *The Rivals*, *The School for Scandal*, and *The Critic*, retains value for the research student because of its detailed Introduction and extensive commentary on the plays. An edition of *The Rivals* prepared by Richard Little Purdy (1935) includes in parallel texts the first manuscript version which was sent to the Stage Licenser and the first printed version.

A number of inexpensive collections of Sheridan's plays have been published, of which the best is the most recent, prepared by Cecil Price (1975) and reproducing the text—though not the full editorial apparatus—of Price's *Dramatic Works* (1973). Both *The Rivals* and *The School for Scandal* have appeared in single volumes suitable for classroom use: the former edited by Alan Downer (1953) and by Cecil Price (1968); the latter edited by John Loftis (1966) and by Cecil Price (1971). Cecil Price has edited *The Letters of Richard Brinsley Sheridan* (1966), with ample commentary that provides reliable biographical information. Sheridan's Parliamentary oratory is reported, though in texts that are not literal transcriptions of what he said, in *Speeches of the Late Right Honourable Richard Brinsley Sheridan*, 'Edited by a Constitutional Friend' (1816). However, his famous orations during the trial of Hastings survive in accurate texts based on the shorthand notes of a person who heard them: *Speeches of the Managers and Counsel in the Trial of Warren Hastings*, ed., A. E. Bond (1859–61).

(II) BIOGRAPHIES

There is no satisfactory biography of Sheridan. Perhaps the best is one of the earliest: Thomas Moore, *Memoirs of the Life of the Right Honourable Richard Brinsley Sheridan* (1825), the value of which is enhanced by the inclusion of passages from Sheridan's preliminary drafts for *The School for Scandal*. Two twentieth-century biographies should be mentioned: Walter Sichel, *Sheridan* (1909), and R. Crompton Rhodes, *Harlequin Sheridan: The Man and the Legends* (1933), both valuable but limited in contrasting manners. Sichel's is long and inclusive and is particularly informative on Sheridan's career in public life, but it is digressive and tedious. Rhodes's is succinct and readable, but it is insufficiently detailed to provide a satisfactory account of the many facets of Sheridan's career.

Several early memoirs and journals by or about other persons are particularly valuable sources of information for Sheridan: his niece Alicia Lefanu's *Memoirs of the Life and Writings of Mrs. Frances Sheridan* (1824), Sheridan's mother; his younger sister Elizabeth's journal, *Betsy Sheridan's Journal* (not published until 1960); the musician Michael Kelly's *Reminiscences* (1826); and James Boaden's *Memoirs of the Life of John Philip Kemble, Esq.* (1825).

(III) CRITICAL STUDIES

Auburn, Mark S., 'The Pleasures of Sheridan's *The Rivals*: A Critical Study in the Light of Stage History,' *Modern Philology*, LXXII (1975), 256–71.

Donohue, Joseph W., Jr., *Dramatic Character in the English Romantic Age.* Princeton, N.J., 1970. Pp. 125–56 are devoted to *Pizarro.*

Jason, Philip K., 'A Twentieth-Century Response to *The Critic,*' *Theatre Survey*, XV (1974), 51–8.

Kaul, Ajodhia Nath, *The Action of English Comedy: Studies in the Encounter of Abstraction and Experience from Shakespeare to Shaw.* New Haven, Conn., 1970. Pp. 131–49 are devoted to Sheridan.

Leff, Leonard J., 'Sheridan and Sentimentalism,' *Restoration and 18th Century Theatre Research*, XII (May 1973), 36–48.

Macey, Samuel L., 'Sheridan: The Last of the Great Theatrical Satirists,' *Restoration and 18th Century Theatre Research*, IX (November 1970), 35–45.

Mudrick, Marvin, 'Restoration Comedy and Later', in W. K. Wimsatt, Jr., ed., *English Stage Comedy.* New York, 1955. Pp. 98–125.

Schiller, Andrew, '*The School for Scandal:* The Restoration Unrestored,' *PMLA*, LXXI (1956), 694–704.

Sprague, Arthur C., 'In Defence of a Masterpiece: "The School for Scandal" Re-examined,' *English Studies Today*, 3rd Series. Ed. G. E. Duthie. Edinburgh, 1964. Pp. 125–35.

(IV) BACKGROUND STUDIES

Baker, Herschel. *John Philip Kemble: The Actor in His Theatre.* Cambridge, Mass., 1942.

Bernbaum, Ernest, *The Drama of Sensibility.* Boston, 1915.

Black, Clementina, *The Linleys of Bath.* Rev. ed., New York, 1926.

Clinton-Baddeley, V. C., *The Burlesque Tradition in the English Theatre After 1660.* London, 1952.

Crane, Ronald S., 'Suggestions Towards a Genealogy of the "Man of Feeling",' *A Journal of English Literary History*, I (1934), 205–30.

Deelman, Christian, 'The Original Cast of *The School for Scandal,*' *The Review of English Studies*, N.S. XII (1962), 257–66.

Downer, Alan S., 'Nature to Advantage Dressed: Eighteenth-Century Acting,' *PMLA*, LVIII, 1002–37.

Fiske, Roger, *English Theatre Music in the Eighteenth Century.* London, 1973.

Friedman, Arthur, 'Aspects of Sentimentalism in Eighteenth-Century

Literature,' in H. K. Miller, E. Rothstein, and G. S. Rousseau, eds., *The Augustan Milieu*. Oxford, 1970. Pp. 247–61.

Gray, Charles Harold, *Theatrical Criticism in London to 1795*. New York, 1931.

Hume, Robert D., 'Goldsmith and Sheridan and the Supposed Revolution of "Laughing" Against "Sentimental" Comedy', in P. W. Korshin, ed., *Studies in Change and Revolution: Aspects of English Intellectual History, 1640–1800*. Menston, Yorkshire, 1972. Pp. 237–276.

Leech, Clifford, and T. W. Craik, general eds., *The Revels History of Drama in English*, Vol. 6: 1750–1880. London, 1975.

The London Stage, 1600–1800: A Calendar of Plays, Entertainments and Afterpieces, together with Casts, Box-Receipts and Contemporary Comment. 5 parts, Carbondale, Ill., 1960–1969. Part IV, ed., G. W. Stone, Jr.: 1747–1776; Part V, ed., C. B. Hogan: 1776–1800.

Lynch, James J., *Box, Pit, and Gallery: Stage and Society in Johnson's London*. Berkeley, Calif., 1953.

Nicoll, Allardyce, *A History of English Drama, 1660–1900*. 6 vols. Cambridge, 1955–59. Vol. III: 1750–1800.

Pedicord, Harry W., *The Theatrical Public in the Time of Garrick*. New York, 1954.

Price, Cecil, *Theatre in the Age of Garrick*. Oxford, 1973.

Quintana, Ricardo, *Oliver Goldsmith: A Georgian Study*. New York, 1967.

Rosenfeld, Sybil, *A Short History of Scene Design in Great Britain*. Oxford, 1973.

Sherbo, Arthur, *English Sentimental Drama*. East Lansing, Mich., 1957.

Smith, Dane Farnsworth, *The Critics in the Audience of the London Theatres from Buckingham to Sheridan*. Albuquerque, N.M., 1953.

Smith, Dane Farnsworth, *Plays About the Theatre in England from . . . 1671 to . . . 1737*. London, 1936.

Tave, Stuart M., *The Amiable Humorist: A Study in the Comic Theory and Criticism of the Eighteenth and Early Nineteenth Centuries*. Chicago, 1960.

Index

S has been used as an abbreviation for Richard Brinsley Sheridan throughout

M